EQUITY

EQUITY

Why Employee Ownership Is Good for Business

Corey Rosen
John Case
Martin Staubus

HARVARD BUSINESS SCHOOL PRESS
BOSTON, MASSACHUSETTS

Library of Congress Cataloging-in-Publication Data
Rosen, Corey M.
    Equity : why employee ownership is good for business / Corey Rosen, John Case, Martin Staubus.
        p. cm.
    ISBN 1-59139-331-0
    1. Employee ownership. 2. Management—Employee participation. I. Case, John, 1944– II. Staubus, Martin. III. Title.
    HD5650.R7345 2005
    658.1'147—dc22

                                                                    2005002388

The paper used in this publication meets the minimum requirements of the American National Standard for Information Sciences—Permanence of Paper for Printed Library Materials, ANSI Z39.48-1992.

*To William Foote Whyte, whose inspiration and vision
set the standard I have hoped to follow.*
—C. R.

*To Patrick, Cecilia, and Maeve: may they live and
work in a more equitable world.*
—J. C.

*To my wife, Elaine, who has made my career in
employee ownership possible.*
—M. S.

CONTENTS

Part One

A DIFFERENT KIND OF COMPANY

Ownership:
The Performance Additive

Stone Construction Equipment is not a company you would automatically pick for survival, let alone prosperity, in today's marketplace.

The company resides in the pleasant but not exactly booming town of Honeoye, in western New York State, a little south of Rochester. It is in a metal-bending, basic-manufacturing business, the kind that has regularly been fleeing American shores for lower-wage and less-restrictive climes. Dick Nisbet, Stone's vice president of manufacturing, wants to be sure that a visitor understands just how unusual his employer's situation has become. "In our industry, we used to have five or six direct competitors in the U.S. that have now been scooped up, bought up, and moved to Mexico."[1] Nisbet is a stolid, plainspoken man in his fifties, a Stone veteran who shakes his head as he rattles off the names of the scooped and the moved. "Multiquip bought up the Essick line, the Whiteman trowel line. They ended up buying the Stow line. Those mixer lines and trowel lines were all made in the U.S.A., and now they're made in Mexico." Multiquip is a substantially larger company, California based, that got its start importing Japanese equipment. It was when Multiquip bought Stow, says Nisbet, that the reality of the situation hit Stone Construction Equipment's two hundred employees. "They've seen the Stow mixer line from Binghamton, New York, get bought up and moved. We're talking 180 miles down the road here. That's close! And by the way, Stow was a formidable competitor of ours for twenty-five years. When we talked at year-end meetings about competition, it was Stow, the guy down there. Well, that guy's gone. All his employees are no longer there. That's gone to Mexico. So it's a reality."

Except that Stone Construction Equipment's reality is different. As this book goes to press, the company is not just surviving, it's a success story. It still employs those two hundred people over three shifts in a long, low factory on Honeoye's broad main street. Aside from the construction downturn after 9/11, it has been growing steadily. It has more than held its own against larger competitors, not only Multiquip but a big German company named Wacker. It is regularly coming out with new products, and it is contemplating a major push into Latin American markets. It is making money.

Stone's secret isn't obvious from a cursory glance around. The plant isn't new. The machines inside are not the latest automated models. The employees are everyday citizens of the rural counties around Honeoye, not recent immigrants desperate for a job at any wage. Nisbet says that, on average, Stone's products cost between 5 percent and 10 percent more than those of competitors. But the price differential hasn't seemed to hurt the business. Customers buy millions of dollars' worth of Stone's cement mixers, buggies, vibrators, compactors, and concrete-finishing equipment every month. Asked in 2003 whether his company could continue to compete with overseas and Mexican production, a shop-floor employee named Stanley Gerhart grinned. "Let's cut to the chase," he replied. "The economy isn't good. We're feeling the pinch same as everybody else. But out of this building, in a backwater town in upstate New York, we're getting the lion's share of what's being sold. We must be doing something right."

The story of Stone Construction Equipment is atypical of today's trends, an anomaly in a sea of shuttered plants and struggling companies. But then Stone is an atypical organization. Its senior leaders—chief executive officer Bob Fien, chief operating officer Lynne Woodworth, Nisbet, and others—run the business along lines that are different from most American companies. They expect Stone's employees to be active partners in the enterprise, not just hired hands. They expect workers throughout the organization to understand and respond to threats and opportunities in the marketplace, coming up with new ideas and better ways of doing things to keep costs low and customers happy. Most of all, they expect employees to learn the business disciplines that are the key to Stone's success, and to use those disciplines to drive growth and profitability. A company in which all these things happen, they argue, will never have to fold up its tent in the face of lower-wage competition.

Employees at a lot of companies might dismiss all those high expectations as so much managerial hot air. But Gerhart and his coworkers are Stone Construction Equipment's owners, a fact that changes matters considerably. They have a sizable stake in the company's long-term prosperity. They are held accountable for their performance not only by the higher-ups but by one another. They get the information they need to make smart decisions on the job, and they have the authority to make them. As we'll see later in this book, Stone is an exemplar of a new model of ownership and management—a model that has become a kind of hotbed of workplace innovation and that seems uniquely suited to the turbulent, topsy-turvy marketplace of the early twenty-first century.

THE NEW EQUITY MODEL

Employee ownership surely counts as one of the more paradoxical phenomena in the business world today. It is astonishingly widespread and enjoys considerable support, yet many businesspeople regard it either as an oddity or as a potential disaster. It typically boosts a company's growth and profitability, yet the myth persists that it can't work or that it somehow hurts employees. When it is taken seriously, as at Stone Construction Equipment, ownership can literally make the difference between going under and surviving, or between just barely getting by and dominating a market niche. Yet even people who should know better—human resources professionals and stock-plan consultants, for example—often view ownership of shares or stock options as just another tool in their kit bag of benefits, and spend their time worrying about technicalities such as accounting rules. They haven't understood just how powerful a notion ownership is or how it is capable of transforming a company.

That kind of transformation is the subject of this book. We will show how Stone and dozens of other companies with extensive employee ownership have built businesses capable of prospering under nearly any condition. We'll try to untangle their secrets, report what they did and how they did it, and extract the lessons for other companies. We'll describe a model of ownership and management—we call it the equity model—that any company can learn, and that can enable its practitioners to achieve what Stone and the others have already achieved. The equity model builds in not only "soft" objectives, such as a spirit of cooperation, but hard-nosed, day-to-day accountability for performance. It enables companies to succeed where others fail because everyone is on the same page, following the same playbook, working toward the same ends. This book will show you what it takes for companies to reach that happy juncture. It will also show you what dramatic improvements such a transformation can bring about.

We think—and we certainly hope—that the audience for these lessons is broad. Tens of thousands of companies all over the world have some kind of employee share ownership plan. Most of them are faced with ever-stiffer competition from all over the globe, and would dearly love their employees to think and act like partners in the enterprise. Indeed, most would probably sell their figurative firstborn children for the kind of initiative and effort shown on shop, store, and office floor by the employee owners you'll meet in this book. But many haven't figured out what it takes to engender those attitudes and behaviors. As we will see, it's a long journey—and employee ownership itself is only the starting point.

But since it *is* the starting point—since it is the indispensable foundation for everything else that we'll be exploring—we'd better begin by dispelling some of the confusion and misconceptions that surround it.

Ubiquity

Employee ownership is no longer a rarity in the United States. The giant Publix Super Market's chain, for example, is owned by its one hundred twenty-one thousand employees. So are many other supermarket companies, ranging in size from a few dozen employees to forty thousand. In fact, a person could eat and drink pretty well by patronizing only food companies with extensive employee ownership. Vermont companies King Arthur Flour and Green Mountain Coffee Roasters fit this bill. So do Schreiber Foods, in Wisconsin, and Bowman Apple Products Company, in Virginia. Full Sail Brewing Company (Oregon) prepares employee-owned beer, as does New Belgium Brewing Company (Colorado). Hot Dog on a Stick, a California fast-food chain whose name reflects its principal product, is 100 percent owned by its two thousand employees. Round Table Pizza, also in California, is 100 percent owned by its three thousand five hundred.

Of course, it isn't just food. Look down any list of companies with an employee stock ownership plan, or ESOP: you'll see contractors and home builders, banks and insurance companies, clothing manufacturers (not to mention world-famous W. L. Gore & Associates, producers of Gore-Tex waterproof fabric), Birkenstock's U.S. distributor and other footwear companies, many printers, at least one mattress maker and one maternity-wear company, scores of retailers (including a variety of home centers, catalog companies, and auto dealers), and many, many service providers, including architectural firms, health-care providers, hotels and resorts, lawn-care companies, and trash haulers. You'll see global-scale industrial suppliers, such as Nypro, Inc., a Massachusetts-based plastics manufacturer with eleven thousand employees in its domestic and international plants, and small specialty firms, such as Rincon Research Corporation, an Arizona company that promises to apply "advanced DSP techniques to signal characterization and identification, spectral analysis, filtering and demodulation, interference cancellation, and signal tracking." Among the largest employee-owned companies in the United States are ACIPCO, an Alabama foundry that is held by a trust for the benefit of its three thousand employees; Journal Communications, owner of the *Milwaukee Journal* and other media properties; CH2M Hill and Parsons Corporation, two of the nation's biggest engineering and construction firms; Graybar Electric, the nation's largest distributor of electrical and telecommunications products; and giant Science Applications International Corporation (SAIC), a $6.7 billion high-technology research and engineering firm that you will read about in this book. Among the smallest are five-employee Union Fish, in Oakland, California, and South Mountain Company, a thirty-employee design/build firm on Martha's Vineyard, an island off the coast of Massachusetts. In June 2003 the dancers at the Lusty Lady cabaret in San Francisco bought out the previous owners, thus making it the first and probably the only employee-owned strip club anywhere.[2]

Our examples so far include only closely held businesses, where much or all of the stock is held by people on the payroll. Another large group of companies is publicly traded—hence primarily owned by outside investors—but with a sizable segment of stock held by a broad base of employees. These companies funnel equity into their workers' hands through a variety of devices. They put company stock into profit-sharing plans and 401(k) retirement accounts. They sponsor both ESOPs and employee stock purchase plans (ESPPs), which allow employees to buy shares at a discount. They hand out stock options or similar equity awards to everyone or nearly everyone, sometimes as performance-related bonuses and sometimes as part of a general distribution. (See the appendix for a taxonomy of the different programs that are available in the United States.) Many of the world's best-known companies go to great lengths to encourage this kind of ownership, with the expectation that employees as a group will wind up holding a significant chunk of the shares. Microsoft has created thousands of millionaires over the years just by distributing options to buy its (once) rapidly appreciating stock; when the company cut back on options grants in 2003, it distributed stock units instead. Procter & Gamble has been giving and selling stock to its employees since 1887 and is now probably between 15 and 20 percent owned by the people who work there.[3] PepsiCo launched an option plan called SharePower in 1989, giving some five hundred thousand employees an annual equity bonus worth 10 percent of their pay; recently the company decreased the number of options but increased the number of shares it distributes. Many—maybe most—large high-technology companies have handed out options or shares to all or nearly all of the people who work for them. In addition to Microsoft, that list includes Intel, Cisco Systems, 3Com Corporation, Verisign, Amazon.com, Adobe, E*TRADE, and hundreds of others. But plenty of non-high-tech companies, such as Starbucks and Southwest Airlines, do the same.

So what are the numbers? Today, about eleven thousand U.S. companies have ESOPs, a specific kind of ownership arrangement. These plans cover an estimated 8.8 million workers, or about 6 percent of the private-sector workforce. (No one is quite sure how many of these companies are wholly or majority owned by their employees; our best guess is that it's a few thousand, employing between 2 and 3 million people.) About two thousand two hundred companies offer their employees 401(k) plans that are primarily invested in the employer's stock; these plans cover some 11 million workers. Another four thousand companies offer stock option plans to an estimated 10 million employees; that group includes the 6 percent of New York Stock Exchange companies that have been providing stock options every year to at least half their employees.[4] Finally, about four thousand companies offer stock purchase plans—those are the plans that allow employees to buy stock at a discount—to some 15.7 million employees. The latter group comprises many of the nation's largest employers, including Wal-Mart Stores, United Parcel Service, IBM, Kroger, and The Home Depot.

Of course, some companies have more than one such plan, and many employees participate in more than one. Overall, roughly 23 million Americans own stock in their employer, and perhaps 10 million own options. If you compare these figures with the number of people who work for companies that have stock—in other words, employees who *can* own stock in their employer—you'll find that about 39 percent are share owners and 17 percent are option holders.[5]

The United States has been a leader in this field, but employee ownership exists in other countries as well. For example:

- Large multinationals have extended ownership plans to their employees around the world. Arthur Andersen (when it was still a firm) found in a 2001 survey of 185 American, British, and Canadian multinationals that 95 percent had some kind of employee share plan and that the vast majority offered the plans globally.

- Several hundred large U.K. companies have some kind of broad ownership plan, as do a few hundred smaller enterprises with American-style ESOPs. In Ireland, large companies such as Aer Lingus, Eircom (the telephone company), and Bord na Mona (a big energy company) offer ESOPs.

- Spain's and Italy's economies include large worker-cooperative sectors. The Mondragón Cooperative Corporation in Spain's

Basque region, to take the best-known example, employs over thirty-five thousand people in a variety of industries and is one of the nation's most successful and admired businesses.

- In new market economies, employee ownership has become a common means of privatizing companies once owned by the state—several hundred in Poland and Russia, for instance, many in Slovenia, and about 150 in Hungary (though many of the latter have subsequently been sold to investors or management).

- The Chinese central government has allowed employees to buy shares in the enterprises it owns—generally the largest and/or the most sensitive businesses—and it has chosen not to intervene in the efforts of several provinces to privatize companies through employee ownership. China's largest multinational company, Huawei Technologies in Shenzen province, is owned by its twenty-two thousand employees. Some Chinese officials indicate that many thousands of businesses are being transformed in this way.

Other employee-ownership experiments are under way in Australia, Egypt, Jamaica, Kenya, and South Africa.

Performance Additive

What's interesting about employee ownership isn't only that it's widespread. It also turns up in a disproportionate number of influential and innovative companies. When last we looked, for example, nearly 80 percent of the corporations on *Fortune*'s "100 Best Companies to Work For" list had some kind of broad-based employee-ownership plan. So did about one-third of the companies on *Inc.* magazine's list of the five hundred fastest-growing privately held businesses. Many ambitious entrepreneurs seem to take it more or less for granted. "We knew we needed employee ownership," a senior executive of upstart airline Jet-Blue Airways recently told a business audience, in a tone suggesting that the reason would be obvious to any dunce. PaeTec Communications, a fast-growing telecommunications business near Rochester, New York, has followed the practice of many young tech companies in passing out options to all employees. Talking to a reporter, executive vice president Dick Ottalagana seemed mystified at the idea that the company would do it any other way. If investors and senior managers took all the stock, he asked a reporter, "what's in it for [the employees]?"[6] At Massachusetts-based Cognex Corporation, the world leader in the technically complex field of industrial machine vision, founder Robert Shillman made a point of keeping much of the stock out of the hands of venture capitalists when the company was young so that he could attract top computer scientists; today the company passes out stock options to all and is 70 percent owned by the people who work there.[7] Ownership can also be an ingredient of successful turnaround efforts. For example, the KPS Special Situations Funds target bankrupt basic-manufacturing companies for acquisition, bringing in new capital, new management, and (typically) a healthy dose of employee ownership. One KPS portfolio company, Blue Ridge Paper Products, Inc., 55 percent owned by KPS and coinvestor GE Capital Corporation, and 45 percent owned by an ESOP, turned profitable not long after it was bought. At last report, its two thousand worker-owners held a collective stake worth $100 million.[8]

None of this should be too surprising, because employee ownership seems to act as a kind of performance booster, often raising a company's growth rates and profitability. The preeminent researchers in this field are professors Joseph Blasi and Douglas Kruse, both of Rutgers, The State University of New Jersey. In 2002 congressional testimony, Kruse summarized the results of some thirty empirical studies, his own and many others, conducted over a twenty-year period, that directly addressed the issue of whether an employee-owned company does as well financially as other companies. Most of the studies on the relationship between employee ownership and company performance found a positive correlation, Kruse reported, though some found no correlation. None found that equity ownership actually hurt business performance. Among the specific findings:

- Companies adopting an ESOP saw between 4 percent and 5 percent higher productivity the year they did so; the higher productivity level was maintained in subsequent years.

- Employee ownership was associated with greater stability of employment, without any corresponding reduction in economic efficiency.

- Employee ownership was linked to faster employment growth, and to higher rates of survival among companies.[9]

Blasi and Kruse came up with similar results when they studied 105 publicly traded companies that implemented a plan providing stock options to at least 75 percent of their employees. These companies improved productivity 17 percent and return on assets 2.3 percent in the three-year period after implementation. In another comparison, the two researchers looked at companies that offered options to at least half their employees, on the one hand, and companies that offered either no plan or a management-only plan, on the other. The broad-based option companies outperformed the others substantially.[10] "While broad-based equity participation within a firm . . . doesn't automatically lead to better performance and attitudes," wrote Kruse in subsequent testimony, "it does help on average to improve productivity, profitability, organizational commitment, and other employee attitudes."[11]

A number of business leaders, notably in high tech, are outspoken fans of employee ownership. "Without the ability to offer stock options," Intel chief executive Craig Barrett told Congress, "many industry leaders today—including Intel—would never have gotten off the ground."[12] Larry Page, cofounder of Google, said, "The significant employee ownership of Google has made us what we are today."[13] Cisco Systems CEO John Chambers goes a step further:

> On employee ownership . . . there's not been a single successful company in the history of high-tech in the last two decades that has done that without broad-based stock option plans. When I originally heard about that in school, I would have called it socialism, when in fact it is the ultimate form of capitalism. It is a very effective way to align interests.[14]

Again, it isn't only people in technology industries. Howard Schultz, founder of Starbucks, pioneered the distribution of options—known at Starbucks as bean stock—in the otherwise transient, low-wage fast-food industry. "The most important thing I ever did was give our partners [employees] bean stock," he told *Fortune*'s Andy Serwer in 2004. "That's what sets us apart and gives a higher-quality employee, an employee that cares more."[15]

Points of Attack

We don't mean to imply that employee ownership always leads to wonderful results or that it enjoys universal support. For one thing, every now and then an employee-owned company fails. When the company in question is big and visible—United Airlines (UAL) is the most recent example—the event typically precipitates declarations that employee ownership *doesn't* work after all. "The imminent bankruptcy of United Airlines may be the final blow to an idea that once entranced both liberals and conservatives," sniffed the conservative commentator Bruce Bartlett of the National Center for Policy Analysis. ". . . As UAL, an employee-owned company, demonstrates, it works a lot better in theory than [in] practice."[16] Such declarations are more than a little mystifying, because employee ownership obviously does work at all the companies mentioned earlier and at thousands more besides. But also: why should anybody conclude from United's experience that employee ownership was the culprit? With equal justice we might conclude from the bankruptcy (twice) of US Airways—and many other conventionally owned airlines over the years—that ownership by the investing public doesn't work. (For more on what went wrong at United, see chapter 4.)

A second point of criticism is that employee ownership depends for its existence on tax breaks and favorable accounting treatment. It's true that the U.S. Congress since the mid-1970s has provided certain tax incentives for companies that set up ESOPs and that the accounting rules governing the plans have at various times provided other financial benefits. The number of ESOPs has waxed and waned modestly over the years as these incentives and rules have been modified in one direction or the other. But so what? Home mortgages get favorable tax treatment, too, because Congress decided that it wanted to encourage home ownership. Congress also wants to encourage employee ownership, and maybe it's right to do so. More importantly, while tax or accounting benefits may persuade a company to consider creating a stock plan, they can't by themselves lead to better performance. Yet that is what ESOPs seem to do.

Stock options, of course, have a history all their own. Companies were using options to reward top executives as early as the 1920s and have done so off and on ever since. But few relied on options to encourage broad-based employee ownership until the rise of the California-based high-technology industry in the last two decades. (This story is well told in the pathbreaking book *In the Company of Owners,* by Joseph Blasi, Douglas Kruse, and Aaron Bernstein.)[17] The use of options proliferated in the 1990s partly because of the example of high tech and partly because companies could distribute them to employees without recording an expense on their income statements. As we write, the international accounting-standards board is about to change that rule, and its U.S. counterpart, known as FASB, has decided to do the same, though the issue has been contentious. So any American business that grants options will have to calculate the value of the options, list this amount as an expense, and thus reduce its reported earnings.[18] As to the likely effects of this change, well, time will tell (and may have already told by the time you read this book). Most research studies indicate that a significant minority of companies will once more restrict options to top executives, although some experts predict that actual practice will change less than these surveys of intentions suggest. Companies may also create other broad-based equity programs to take the place of options, as Microsoft and PepsiCo have already done. But it is unlikely that employee ownership overall will shrink significantly.

The most cogent criticism—though also off the mark, in our view—is that employee ownership jeopardizes workers' retirement security. The collapse of Enron, and the obliteration of the stock value held in Enron employees' retirement accounts, for example, led to outcries in the media and in Congress: *there oughta be a law* against companies loading up those accounts with their own stock, thus making workers vulnerable to management malfeasance. Owning stock in your employer "is one of the most serious problems that hasn't gotten the attention it deserves," said Alicia Munnell, director of the Center for Retirement Research at Boston College. "It's so imprudent to have your investments in the same spot as your human capital."[19]

Munnell's point is well taken: nobody approaching retirement wants to hold only one stock in his or her portfolio. Recognizing this, the U.S. government requires companies with ESOPs to offer diversification opportunities as their employees reach age fifty-five and ten years of plan participation. Employees can thus swap their company stock for other assets to be held in their account. The vast majority—more than 80 percent—of ESOP companies themselves recognize the danger, and so make a point of offering conventional diversified 401(k) plans or other diversified retirement programs to everyone, in addition to the ESOP. In fact, companies with ESOPs are much *more* likely than others to offer 401(k)s, as well as profit-sharing and pension plans. Employees thus might have a sizable portion of their retirement nest eggs in their employer's stock but hold another sizable portion in diversified mutual funds. Enron was a poor model of employee ownership, because it pushed the employees to bear too much risk. Unfortunately, Enron wasn't alone. While ESOPs are generally offered as part of a retirement package, many public companies provide *only* 401(k) plans, and about half the employees in these plans can invest in company stock, have their own investments matched with company stock, or both. Of this group, research by the National Center for Employee Ownership found that 43 percent had more than 20 percent of their assets in company stock—probably too much concentration in a single asset, if the 401(k) plan is all they are counting on for retirement.

Anyway, there's another aspect of ownership that needs to be mentioned in this context. Ownership entails risk, of course. No one has yet figured out how to create a business that is assured of prosperity. But ownership can also bring enormous rewards. If you worked (at the right time!) for Microsoft, Cisco Systems, or any of the many other fast-growing companies that provided options to most of their employees, the chances are good that your retirement is secure. And even if you didn't, you may be in pretty good shape, provided that your company had some form of employee ownership. A few years ago, when the government was investigating retirement plans as a result of the Enron debacle, the ESOP Association (a trade organization for ESOP companies) surveyed its members to ask whether their employees had been able to build up comfortable nest eggs. About 50 percent of the 250 responding companies said that their plans were less than five years old, and so people had not had time to accumulate substantial accounts. But dozens of other companies reported rather astonishing stories. McKay Nursery Company, in Wisconsin, had recently distributed some $2 million to four retiring blue-collar employees. (McKay, which, like many agricultural companies, relies heavily on seasonal labor, includes migrant workers in its stock-ownership plan.) The RLI Corporation, a specialty insurance company in Illinois, reported that the average employee held an account balance worth ten times his or her annual salary. Beacon Technologies, in Georgia, said that a recently retired employee had never earned more than $30,000—but that his stock cash-out netted him $450,000. Garney Companies, a heavy construction company based in Missouri, said that one laborer had worked for seventeen years, had become a superintendent, and now had more than $1 million in his account.

In the course of research for this book, one of us (John Case) visited Scot Forge, an open-die forge shop headquartered in Spring Grove, Illinois, about an hour northwest of Chicago. Among the people John talked to was Leo Szlembarski, a lathe operator who had been with Scot for thirty-four years. Like Stone Construction Equipment, Scot is 100 percent owned by its employees, and Szlembarski said it was not uncommon for blue-collar workers to retire with $700,000 or $800,000 in their stock accounts. He himself, he confided, had "a little more." When a business fails, employee ownership can certainly compromise employees' retirement security. When it succeeds, as Scot and the other companies mentioned earlier did, it *provides* retirement security. That's part of the point.

Ironically, the most telling weakness of employee ownership as an idea isn't that it doesn't work—it works fine—or that it jeopardizes employees' retirement, which it does only when it is poorly implemented (as at Enron). The most telling weakness is that at some companies it just doesn't generate much excitement. The people who implement employee-ownership plans—small-company owners, large-company human resources or finance professionals—often treat the whole thing as just another benefit or financial tool. They don't encourage managers to run the business any differently. They don't talk to employees about what it might mean to be an owner, or change their expectations about how people approach their jobs. When that's the case, employees view ownership accordingly. Sure, the ESOP might be nice—but it's no more inspiring or transforming than a 401(k) retirement plan. Sure, options are fine—but unless the stock is rising rapidly, maybe we'd prefer to have cash. When nobody makes a big deal about ownership, not surprisingly, ownership has little effect on a business's performance.

This is a missed opportunity of staggering proportions. It scarcely needs repeating: we live and work these days in a world of constant business challenges. Companies compete on a global scale. They face loss of pricing power and shrinking margins. Yet they must somehow attract and keep high-quality employees—who, more than ever, want rewarding work and a stake in what they do. Done right, employee ownership can transform a business into one that is capable of meeting these challenges. It can enable companies to tap an immense reservoir of energy, intelligence, and extra effort from people throughout the organization. It can get everyone focusing on the same goals and working toward the same objectives. It can lead to quantum leaps in a company's performance, not to mention in employee satisfaction.

We have seen this happen again and again. For the last couple of decades, each of us has studied, visited, written about, and consulted to companies that have extensive employee ownership. We have listened to senior executives, middle managers, and frontline workers talk about how it works in practice and what it means to them. In preparation for this book, we gathered together our own and others' research on the subject, and we read widely in the history of employee ownership and other efforts to reshape the workplace. Then we set out on journeys around the country to find some of the companies that were doing it best. We spent time at many such companies, interviewing people from all walks of life within the organizations. We realized that, though every company was different, there were common principles that united them—principles that amounted to a fundamentally new way of structuring and running a business. These companies seemed to have begun with the idea of ownership and taken it to a higher level.

So here is what you will find in the chapters that follow. First we want to return to Stone Construction Equipment, see up close how it operates, and let you hear directly from the people who work there. We'll compare Stone with some of the other companies that are the pioneers of this new approach, and we'll try to extract what they all have in common. Then we'll ask where this new approach to management came from—and to answer that question, we'll review the rich, fascinating history of employee ownership and participative management. In chapters 5, 6, and 7, we'll get to the hands-on part. We'll explore in depth how a variety of companies have done it: how they have begun with employee ownership and gone on to create a new and more effective way of running a business. Overall, the book will show you the key elements of a new model of management—a model created and implemented by these companies and others and that right now is enabling them to outperform their competitors.

We're calling it the equity model because it relies on equity in both senses of the word. Employees are shareholders—equity owners—in their businesses. And they work in an equitable environment, where people's contributions to the company's performance are valued no matter what their job, and where everyone shares in the rewards. "Those who contribute to the company should own it" is one of the favorite sayings of J. Robert (Bob) Beyster, founder of SAIC, a company you will read about in chapter 5, and a pioneer of employee ownership. His words could be taken as the epigram for this book.

The Equity Model

Stone Construction Equipment traces its ancestry back to a company called Stone Conveyor, established by a man named Guthrie Stone. In 1967 Guthrie's son Al took over the small construction-equipment shop and set up a new business to make cement mixers. The new company didn't do badly. In 1971 it hit $1 million in sales. By 1974 its six-, seven-, and eight-cubic-foot mixers had become something of an industry standard. In 1976 its sales were $5 million. The company branched out into motorized trowels and other concrete-finishing equipment. It bought state-of-the-art machining equipment for the factory, and it won a patent on a clutch system for those trowels. In 1979 Al Stone sold 2 percent of the stock to an employee stock ownership plan, or ESOP, which would hold it in trust for workers' retirement. In 1980 he brought in a marketing vice president named Bob Fien, with the thought that Fien might one day take over as chief executive.

But a couple of years later, for personal reasons, Al Stone decided he wanted to sell the business. Prospective buyers began touring the plant, and Stone's employees began feeling nervous. Fien proposed that, instead of selling to an outsider, Stone sell his stock to the ESOP. It's a common enough transaction in the United States: an ESOP borrows money to buy a company and then distributes stock to employee retirement accounts as the loan is paid off. Al was intrigued. The tax benefits were attractive. Fleet Bank was willing to provide financing. Fien would be taking over as president only a little ahead of schedule. So Al agreed. By 1985 he had sold 30 percent of his shares to the ESOP. In 1986 he sold the rest, and from that time forward the employees of Stone Construction Equipment were sole owners of their company.

Bob Fien—the name is pronounced Feen—hadn't come to Stone with that plan in mind. But he might as well have. Born in 1932, Fien had grown up in Rochester, the son of a factory worker. At the University of Rochester he had studied management, becoming a disciple of the philosophy known as Theory Y. Theory Y, which calls for an empowered, engaged workforce, had been developed by the management theorist Douglas McGregor, author of the classic book *The Human Side of Enterprise*. McGregor contrasted his Theory Y with Theory X, the traditional command-and-control model associated with Frederick W. Taylor's ideas about scientific management. Theory X assumed employees were difficult to motivate and had little to contribute by way of useful ideas or information. McGregor argued that if you engaged people enough, they would help find ways to make their work more productive and efficient.

Before coming to Stone, Fien had served as president of two troubled companies—a publishing firm in San Francisco and a manufacturer of costume jewelry in Rochester—and had turned them both around, using the precepts of Theory Y. He was now ready to put his ideas about empowerment to work in a growing manufacturing business. Employee ownership seemed to lay appropriate groundwork, but no more. "It was obvious to me, being 100 percent employee owned by itself was nothing," he said recently. Alone, "it didn't mean a damn thing. We had to change the culture."

So Fien embarked on a mission to transform the outlook and attitudes of his company's employees. Stone Construction Equipment wasn't an unusually adversarial place—it had no union, for example—but neither was it a model of enlightened management. "When I came in [in 1976], the theory at Stone's was, come in, punch your time clock, go do your job, and that's it," recalled Stanley Gerhart. "'You do what we tell you. We don't want to hear your ideas. You just do your job.' The buzzer rings when you go to break, the buzzer rings when you go back to work. The whole scenario. 'Build a million of this and don't stop till we tell you.' The old philosophy."

Fien sent all his managers to classes with an industrial psychologist to learn a more respectful way of dealing with the people they supervised. (Up to then, he says, "they yelled.") He began talking to employees, sharing information about the company and asking for ideas about improving things. He did away with time clocks. ("Time clocks convey the idea that you don't trust a person to write down when they come in. So we had a big party where they smashed the time clocks.") He abolished the quality-control department and asked employees to begin checking their own work. He sent not just managers but nearly everyone in the plant to classes where they could learn the techniques of "lean" manufacturing, the production system developed and pioneered at Toyota. The whole thing was a long, hard slog. Some of the managers didn't take kindly to the new approach and barked out orders the way they always had. Some employees figured they now owned the company and didn't need to show up for work every day. When Fien tried to talk to production employees about the company's financials—literally walking them through the income statement in a series of meetings—he saw heads begin to nod. But they weren't nodding assent, they were dozing off.

Still, Fien kept at it. He introduced monthly meetings to go over just a few key financial numbers. He asked people to form committees to take on responsibilities such as preventive maintenance on the machines. He added niceties such as "thank you" tags on every piece of equipment, signed by the last person who checked it over. If a customer called to complain about a piece of equipment, he or she could talk with the people who built it—and those people would go out to fix it if necessary. Eventually he organized production workers into work cells, each one charged with a particular set of tasks; the cells would meet daily to go over the day's work, trade ideas, and raise questions or concerns. All these innovations soon began paying off. *Industry Week* named Stone one of the ten best manufacturing plants in America. The company introduced major new products, such as a line of ride-on asphalt rollers. It built an addition to the factory, asking shop-floor employees to give advice about how to configure the space. Sales climbed steeply and in 1998 topped $40 million. But a funny thing was happening: the head count, which had peaked at more than three hundred, began dropping with attrition. People were finding ways to produce more with less labor. By the end of the century, Stone was down to about two hundred and holding. Its sales fell during the 2001–2002 downturn but picked up again in 2003. Still, there was no talk of adding people.[1]

ON THE SHOP FLOOR

To go inside the Stone Construction Equipment plant and talk with employees is to understand some pieces of this puzzle, and indeed to see in day-to-day operation the different methods of management that we are calling the equity model. The tour takes you through engineering and customer service; out onto the shop floor, where sheet steel and components arrive on the loading dock and are turned into machinery; past the parts department; and back again to the office.

In engineering, Scott Woodruff demonstrates software that allows Stone to cut as many parts as possible from a single sheet of steel. Woodruff developed the software himself. "We entertained buying a program outside, but Scott and others sent them a typical print," explains Dick Nisbet. "They laid out all the parts and got them all on a five-by-ten sheet. But Scott got them on a four-by-eight. So we didn't buy the software package; we kept Scott." Woodruff taught himself most of the programming he knows. Not long ago, he noticed that a redesigned bag splitter—a piece of serrated metal attached to the company's cement mixer, designed to do what its name implies—could be squeezed onto a part of the sheet that would otherwise be scrap. So he designed a new one and began incorporating it. "No one told Scott to reduce scrap," says Lynne Woodworth, the company's chief operating officer. "He saw an opportunity and did it on his own."

Out on the shop floor, Freddy Johnson runs a computer-controlled plasma arc cutting machine (made by Hypertherm, as it happens—another company with extensive employee ownership). The cutting machine takes instructions from Woodruff's software and slices the sheet of steel into usable parts. Johnson shows several small inventions he and his coworkers have come up with to make their jobs easier and to check the quality of their output: a homemade go/no-go gauge, an adjustable grinding table, a new cutting fluid that keeps parts cleaner and needs to be changed less frequently. Overhead is a recently purchased $40,000 cranc that lifts the heavy steel sheets. Dissatisfied with the trouble and risk of using the plant's big crane for the job, as they did before, Johnson and other operators found out how much this smaller one would cost, figured in the advantages for safety, and showed management how much time the new crane would save. Buying it was a no-brainer. "We just bring the stuff up," says Johnson, referring to the ideas that regularly are batted about by his work cell. "We talk about it, cost it out. We try to figure out what's the best bang for our buck. And if it's worth doing, we go ahead and do it." Safety is a primary concern, not just because "we don't like getting hurt" but because it saves the company workers' compensation costs. "If we don't get hurt, we don't have to do the [insurance] claims, and we keep that cost down. When it costs the company money, that means there's that much less money I can make."

Today's management literature, of course, is filled with anecdotes much like these—stories of empowered employees taking initiative, thinking and acting like owners of their company, even if they often aren't. The stories often provoke skepticism: how long are people really going to keep on behaving like that if there's nothing in it for them? But at Stone Construction Equipment the employees *are* owners, with stock piling up in their retirement accounts, and acting as such seems utterly ingrained. Nearly everyone offers examples like those just mentioned—something somebody did, on his or her own initiative, to improve things. Two employees volunteer to go to Mexico to fix a shipment that arrived in disarray. A team shaves a tenth of an hour off mixer production by deciding to put a mixer's tires on after painting rather than before. In the literature, the lesson typically stops at this point, as if business success somehow stems purely from a change in attitude and small everyday process improvements. Fien never bought that notion. Yes, he said, the culture is cool. Yes, the positive attitudes and process improvements developed by people such as Woodruff and Johnson are critically important. But equally important are the disciplines that govern the company's daily operation. These include a systematic long-range planning process; annual operating plans and timelines deriving from the long-range goals, with tight monthly checkpoints; a prescribed process for introducing new products; close management of sales accounts; and so on.

The key discipline seems to be an approach to production—lean manufacturing, as done at Toyota—that enables Stone Construction

Equipment to do things most of its competitors simply can't. Sheet steel arrives on the loading dock several times a day in small quantities; there is no warehouse. Parts are produced through what's known as a kanban system; each part needed by a workstation is "stockpiled" in two one-man pushcarts, and when assemblers find that one cart is empty, it goes back to the fabrication shop to be refilled. Stone forecasts demand, of course, and plans its overall capacity accordingly. But it does not build to forecast, it builds to order. It can take a customer's order for a customized ride-on compactor, painted green, on Tuesday, and ship the compactor out on Friday. It can crank out individually ordered smaller products such as mixers in twenty-four hours or less. Stone has thirteen product lines, more than 375 possible configurations within those lines, and endless possibilities for customization (for example, through different colors). Order a Stone Construction Equipment machine today, and you can have it—precisely as you ordered it—a few days later. Fien and Woodworth believe that this ability is the company's key competitive edge. It is a hard-to-emulate advantage that sets Stone apart and that has enabled it to prosper in a brutal market.

What makes the system work, however, isn't just the Toyota-style techniques, it's the willingness of Stone's employees to function in a manner that traditional manufacturing employees, accustomed to doing the same jobs day in and day out, would find astonishing. At 12:45 every day, Nisbet's factory supervisors, known as coaches, gather in a meeting room to plan production for the next twenty-four hours and to draft people to go to the departments where they're needed the rest of that day and the following morning. Throughout the day, each department has brief "huddles" to ascertain where they stand against the day's goals and to redeploy people as necessary. Virtually all the employees are cross-trained so that they can switch easily from welding to assembly to painting to something else. The job of figuring out how to meet a day's constantly shifting production goals is theirs, as much as it is any manager's. "The people on the floor get involved, so much involved that you wouldn't believe," says Stanley Gerhart. "I might say, 'Hey, I can get those two guards later; why don't you let me go get the robot parts; then I can run over and do the guards.' And another guy'll say, 'I'm gonna be OK for a while, Stanley; why don't you run over and get the robot, and I'll do the guards.' All these people put their heads together to come up with that thing at the end of the day." Whiteboards in each department track what needs to be done, who's responsible for doing it, and how things are going so far. "What you've got is each operator's name," says Nisbet, pointing to a board in the machine shop. "You see the 'one-third' sign up? That's a third of a day. They're going to do a checkpoint, like the quarters in football, and come back together for a three- to five-minute huddle at the third period." He gestures toward the board, which includes the notation "Joe—3." "Joe signed up to make three parts today by the first third. And he'll report at the huddle, 'I got three, or I got four, or I got two and a half and I'm in trouble making my signup today, so we might need to adjust the teams.' That's what you're seeing up there."

Nor does the involvement stop at the department door; people find other things to do while, for example, a milling machine is doing its work. Nisbet continues:

> The other thing we do in the machine shop is while we're milling, they see opportunities in other departments. They'll assemble gearboxes, they'll do the lower part of rammers out here, which in the old days were assembly jobs. So now they're taking advantage of their cycle time and actually doing more work to reduce the cost of that product. If you think about it, they are actually putting no [scheduled] time toward that job. Their actual time is toward this part that they're making, and so you're getting that one free.

In a conventional company, he adds, none of that would happen, because employees would complain loudly. "'You're making me do more work!' Well no, we're not. The guys, because of the involvement, the education, they are seeing the opportunity and bringing that to the bottom line."

That approach—everyone pitching in to figure out exactly what needs doing—seems to permeate Stone Construction Equipment, and not just on the factory floor. People in customer service huddle up at the start of the day to check on outstanding orders. People in the parts department watch the fax as it spews out the day's orders, and if necessary will call in a person or two from the shop to help fill them. Sally Schinsing runs the print shop, which produces product manuals and marketing materials, also on a just-in-time basis. "When we have corporate mailings, she will actually draft players from the organization—marketing folks, production folks—and when she's done, she sends them back," says Nisbet.

Stone's methods have their drawbacks. "It's a very, very fast pace," acknowledged Gerhart, who is in his fifties. He sometimes worries that he won't be able to keep up. "I'm an old man in a young man's game." Nor does every last employee buy into the equity model. A welder named Burt Farley, asked to talk to a visitor, declared firmly that Stone was "not the Shangri-la that Bob [Fien] might want you to think it is," and said that he himself worked at his own pace regardless of the daily goals. "Sometimes their expectations are a little more than I care to do, and I don't feel bad about that." Farley didn't even buy the idea that he was "really" an owner. "This company is really no different than any other company, is it? The ESOP is nothing to me until I get ready to retire. Until then I work for The Man." On the other hand, Farley reported that he had been at Stone twenty-four years, held roughly $100,000 worth of equity in the business, and considered the company a "good place to work." He may be a reminder that no management system can please all of the people all of the time.

But Stone Construction Equipment—the company—is a reminder that Americans don't necessarily have to cede every manufacturing job to lower-wage competitors. Because they have found a different way of working together, Farley, Gerhart, and the others still have jobs. The people who worked for Stow, 180 miles down the road in Binghamton, do not.

THE "EQUITY ATTITUDE"

The central phenomenon we observed in the businesses we visited—in fact, it may be the defining characteristic of an equity company—is a particular attitude, a turn of mind that most of the people at Stone Construction Equipment seem to have taken to heart. It might be described with the phrase *This is* our *company, and we will do whatever is necessary to help it succeed*. This attitude shouldn't be idealized or taken lightly. It is difficult to engender and to maintain. It typically entails a ton of hard work and extra effort. Like any business owners, employee owners in these companies are rarely idle. They put in off-the-clock hours. They keep a sharp eye out every day for ways to save a nickel or bring in another dollar. They worry about what to do when the numbers don't look right. They do not say, "That's not my job" when something needs doing; they plunge in and do it. "When a machine operator left W. L. Gore last year," wrote *Time*'s Laird Harrison in 2002, "the human resources department naturally began looking for a replacement." Then before anyone got as far as posting a want ad, the man's former team members met and figured out how they could make do with one less body. They would have to work harder without more pay, but they wanted to do what was best for the enterprise. Said Gore human resources associate Sonia Dunbar, "That doesn't happen at other companies."[2]

But of course it does happen at companies that, like W. L. Gore & Associates, take equity ownership seriously. In fact, we heard versions of this attitude not only at Gore—see chapter 6—but at companies large and small, in many different industries, from veteran employees and those more recently hired, from professionals with PhD's, from managers with (and without) MBA's, and from frontline workers with high school educations.

Take the twenty-plus people who work at the King Arthur Flour retail store in Norwich, Vermont, just off Interstate 91 and across the river from Hanover, New Hampshire. One of the oldest companies in America, King Arthur has metamorphosed over the last several years from a producer and distributor of high-grade flour to a specialty company that caters to amateur and professional bakers. It sells its wares—flours, mixes, baking implements, and the like—over the Web and through a catalog as well as through retail outlets. Its own retail store and baking-instruction center have become a destination for baking aficionados, a pint-sized version of what L.L. Bean, for example, is to outdoors enthusiasts and fashionistas. King Arthur is 100 percent owned by its 150 employees, and store manager Cindy Fountain describes what it's like to run a retail outlet in which everyone is an owner:

> We're employee owners here. We're all partners in providing
> our customers with a retail experience that they will enjoy, be
> comfortable with, remember. Opening the doors is one of my

favorite times of the day. My team leaders and I get in a huddle. We determine what's going to happen that day. We discuss the budget number for the day, where we need to be at the end of the day . . . Cindy Johnson, she's the one on the sales floor. She needs to know, three hours into the day, OK, a quarter of our sales are there. At noon, are we halfway there or not? And she can make the call: we're a little under budget today, does anybody want to go home? Or, gee, we're busier than we thought we were, a bus came in we weren't expecting, can you spend an extra couple of hours? The employees are absolutely flexible . . . because we own the company. Doesn't mean I won't be grouchy and tired sometimes, but I own the company.

We don't have a laundry service. We take our dirty towels out of the kitchen every day and take them home. Susan Miller takes all the things that are used in the baking-education center home and washes them. It's crazy, but it's true . . . Cindy Johnson does all our gift certificates—getting an envelope, putting a catalog in it, putting a gift certificate into it, making a pretty presentation. We're very proud of the store, and the company. As the manager, having a team of employee owners actually makes my job easier. A few times a year, we host storewide sales, and these sales require more staff than usual. I have never had a problem asking staff to come in early to help prepare, to stay late to help close, or even add an extra shift if necessary. As a company of employee owners, the response is always, "What can I do to help?"

Or listen to David Snyder, of SAIC, which is about as far away from King Arthur as you can get. His company, headquartered in San Diego, California, is a *Fortune* 500 giant, with close to $7 billion in revenue and more than forty thousand employees. It is almost wholly owned by present and former employees through a variety of broad-based stock-ownership programs that we will discuss in chapter 5. Snyder, an MIT graduate with a master's in economics from UCLA, has had a long business career with high-tech firms and since 2000 has been director of business development for SAIC. His job is to license technologies developed by SAIC scientists and engineers into the commercial sector:

It's astonishing to me. A company our size, being as far-flung as it is, I routinely communicate with people by e-mail or telephone, some of whom I've never met. And yet I hear the same words coming out of everyone's mouth: "As an employee owner," they say, "I think we should protect our intellectual property this way." Or "We should try to get some extra money for ourselves that way," or "We should watch that expense." That phrase always comes out: "As an employee owner, I think . . ." It's almost like a code word.

This may sound weird, but I treat my own job like my own little business. Every day—and I don't mean that figuratively or metaphorically—every day I ask myself, "What am I going to do today that's really valuable from a dollars-and-cents point of view?" All too often, working in an office, you get caught up in "I'm busy therefore I'm productive." [laughs] But if I only work ten minutes a day and I have brought in $10 million during those ten minutes, that would be a good day. It's the value of what you do. That's what I try to focus on.

John Cain is chief executive officer of Scot Forge, a five-hundred-employee open-die forge shop with three locations northwest of Chicago; in keeping with company tradition, he likes to wear a bright tartan sport coat to work. Scot, which is wholly owned by its employees, converts raw steel into huge rings and other shapes that are used in heavy industrial machinery and defense applications. What matters most to many of Scot's customers, Cain explains, is delivery time: if they have a machine that is down because a big gear must be replaced, they can't afford to wait a minute longer than is absolutely necessary. So Scot prides itself on getting the job done when the customer needs it:

And even if it's something that's not a typical lead time, if you have to short-cycle that thing, we will work Sundays. It's not a management thing; it doesn't take any involvement from me at all to get that done. If I come in Sunday and just walk through to see what's going on, there are two or three machines running. I'll go up and talk to [the operators]; they'll know everything about the customer, the job, where it's going, why they need to be there doing it . . . No one has to come in here and get overtime approved. And no one says, "Well, is it worth it to me giving up my weekend to keep the customer satisfied?" They understand this as an owner; in business you're here to serve customers. They find ways to share the load and share the time . . . They might work a shorter shift: maybe they can come in and work four hours at a time, or three, four guys will come in and get it done instead of one guy having to spend the whole weekend. We don't say, "You gotta work Saturday" or "You gotta work Sunday." They know better how to get it done. We owe them the information so that they can figure out the best way to get it done. Many times they come up with a plan to get it accomplished without having to work through a weekend.

Tom Allison, a heat-treat operator who has been with Scot four years, explains why he thinks people at the company work this way:

I guess if you're an employee and you understand you own a part of it, you're going to work harder for yourself than you are for someone else. Because someone else is going to be making the money, and you're doing the work for them. Here you're doing the work for yourself. It all comes back to that . . . I would say that if I was at any job, I would give 100 percent. But you feel much better when you come here and you're working for yourself. It's good to see the guys around you all giving 100 percent [too].

And John Kasprzak, a machinist who has been with Scot five years, describes how he personally approaches his job:

We're an employee-owned company. We care, and we're watching what people around us are doing . . . For myself, in my job, I'm always looking for things that I can do faster. Be more profitable. Be more profitable. The more profit we can bring in on this machine I'm running, the more my shares are worth, the better my retirement is going to be. The bigger my dividends are going to be. All those things, they're all based on how we work and how everything goes. And just being effective and efficient.

It should be noted that this attitude turns a couple of centuries of capitalist history on its head. Employee ownership and equity-based management, if we can call it that, establish a rough unity of interest between management and labor, and between owners and employees. It puts people who traditionally have fought with each other, or at least regarded one another with perpetual mistrust, on the same team. Brad Bartholomew, a Southwest Airlines captain who has written extensively on airline labor relations—and who, like virtually all Southwest employees, holds stock in the company—succinctly describes the difference in his industry between the conventional model and the equity model. The former model

> ... basically says management's job is to handle everything associated with the company's success and labor's job is to fight to get what it can from the company ... Following this path generates little talk or concern with making the total pie bigger. Labor relations and profitability are consistently ugly. [The latter model] ... says both management and labor are sailing on the same ship and must find a way to work together—sharing in the setbacks and the booty. On this path there is a genuine shared focus on making the pie bigger. Labor and management work cooperatively to find solutions and implement them together. Both sides feel a sense of pride, uniqueness, and ownership. Disagreements and heated arguments do sometimes occur, but they are not resolved by fighting.[3]

THE THREE ELEMENTS OF THE EQUITY MODEL

So how does a company reach the point where most employees share this attitude? That's where the specifics of ownership and management come in—how the business is structured and how it is run. None of the companies we studied followed exactly the same path. But the research and interviewing suggest that there are three key elements and that without all of them, it won't work. One element is equity itself—stock ownership significant enough that it matters to employees' financial future. The second is a culture that helps people think and feel like the owners they are. The third, and often overlooked, element is a shared understanding of key business disciplines, and a common commitment to pursuing them. We'll briefly examine each element of the model here and then return to them in considerably more detail in chapters 5, 6, and 7.

Equity Ownership

Ownership is indispensable because it is what tips the balance of the conventional employment equation.

Traditionally, those who provide the capital to a company own the entire business. Management is accountable to these owners and to nobody else. While owners can lose their money if the business goes south, they have a claim on *all* the earnings and *all* the growth in equity value if it succeeds. So their interest in the company's growth and profits is paramount. If you weren't born with the talents of a Michael Jordan or a Madonna, and if you didn't happen to choose wealthy parents, this is how you can get truly rich—by investing in and building a successful business.

If you are a traditional business owner, however—and if your company is larger than a one-person or one-couple operation—you face a time-honored challenge. You must pursue growth and profits through a workforce of employees who do not share your interest in growth and profits. Of course, employees have an interest in seeing that the company fares well enough that it does not close its doors and eliminate their jobs. And if it grows, *maybe* they can earn more money or get a better position. But the connection between business success and their own is at best tenuous and uncertain. So unless the company is in dire straits, why on earth should they exert themselves unnecessarily to make sure that it succeeds and prospers? Why should they come up with time-saving ideas or productivity improvements? Indeed, why should middle managers listen if they do? As Tom Allison observes, "Someone else is going to be making the money."

Modern management has recognized this divergence of interests and has created a whole kit bag of carrots and sticks to address it. Employees get frequent performance reviews, always backed by the threat of dismissal. They are subjected to motivational speeches and team-building exercises, in hopes that they will be inspired to perform better (and not look for a job somewhere else). They are "incented" with bonuses, merit raises, and prospects of promotion. Readers who serve in corporate human resource departments will recognize themselves as the keepers of these kit bags and no doubt can talk intelligently about how their own company uses a judicious combination of both sanctions and stimulants. But whatever an individual company's mix, the expectation is that employees will not move forward to pursue corporate growth and profits without them. The expectation is often clearest in unionized settings, because of the overtly adversarial system of labor-management relations that has been part of American law since early in the last century. The strike and the lockout are this system's quintessential weapons: each says, in effect, *we on our side are willing to damage the company*, where our joint interests lie, in order to further our own interests at the expense of yours.

In principle, employee ownership transforms this dynamic because it gives everyone in the company a direct and visible interest in the longer-term success of the business. From top management to the front lines, the participants in employee-owned companies are partners in enterprise, sharing a single agenda and common goals. But note that we said "in principle." In practice, the traditional assumption of conflicting interests does not disappear overnight. Changing it depends partly on *how much* equity employees own. Sporadic gifts of one hundred stock options, or a few shares added to 401(k) retirement accounts each year, are unlikely to make the recipients recalculate their economic interests. Substantial holdings, however—holdings that grow significantly from year to year—may do just that. Change also depends on education that helps employees understand the implications of their equity ownership. This is a theme we'll return to repeatedly in this book.

These not-too-surprising truths are reflected in a common perception at equity-based companies, which is that it often takes a while for new employees to "get it"—to realize that they actually are co-owners of the business—and that one key element in getting it is simply watching the value of their holdings mount. Here is Karen Garsson, director of stock programs at giant SAIC:

> I think there are a number of people, to be honest with you, to whom ownership doesn't mean a lot at Day One . . . But ownership is a core part of our company, and over time we see that

folks really start to understand it. The light goes on after a while, and people begin to value the opportunity to own part of the company they work for.

And here is John Czerwinski, who works in a sales role at W. L. Gore & Associates, which with approximately seven thousand employees is still one of the larger employee-owned companies:

> I've watched a lot of new people come in. It really surprises you, because they're very capable, very savvy; they talk about Gore and what we offer. The ASOP [associate stock ownership plan]? It's "Yeah, yeah, I know we've got the ASOP." And then you talk to the same person two, three, four years later, and it's like, "Holy cow, I never really understood what you were talking about." I've had a lot of people all of a sudden say, "OK, this is an interesting horse to ride." Because they could see, ching ching, they could see something was really happening to them.

It doesn't seem to matter, incidentally, what percent of a given company's stock any single employee owns. For larger companies—particularly those that are publicly traded—the percentage owned by employees as a group is usually small (less than 20 percent) anyway. What does matter is the size of the stockholding as compared with an employee's personal financial expectations. You feel like an owner when what you own feels like a significant asset.

But while an ownership interest of real financial substance is necessary, it is hardly sufficient. The way a company goes about its business needs to change in key ways as well. If it grants plenty of stock but then says in so many words, "Now back to work as usual," it will get results as usual. What it has to do instead is create an environment—a culture—in which people come to feel like the owners they are.

Ownership Culture

The typical "culture" at conventional companies—the norms and expectations that govern what people do every day on the job—has evolved considerably over the past couple of decades. Employees and managers were once part of a rigid hierarchy. They did what they were told to do by those above them in the chain of command, and they didn't ask questions. The hierarchy was reinforced by different expectations relating to dress, hours, freedom to come and go, pay and bonuses, parking spaces, office size, job titles, and a dozen other indications of power and status. More recently, many companies have tried to soften the hierarchy. They have done away with some status distinctions (no reserved parking spaces, no executive lunchroom). They have preached that "people are our most important assets," and have exhorted employees to use their brains as well as their hands. They have announced that they wanted their employees to have a "sense of ownership," even when no actual equity ownership was available to employees. (This is a bit like taking hungry people into a restaurant to give them a "sense of lunch," without allowing them to order anything.) Line managers, of course, didn't always buy into such high-minded pronouncements. They had reached their current positions because they were good at telling people what to do, and they weren't about to change now. Most employees remained pretty skeptical as well, for the reason outlined earlier: most of the benefits were still going to someone else.

Equity companies usually resemble these conventional businesses in some respects. They have presidents and chief financial officers. They have middle managers and supervisors. But they can alter the assumptions of hierarchy far more dramatically, simply because the underlying economic reality is different. Employees find the idea of acting like owners less hypocritical and therefore more appealing. Managers may find it somewhat more difficult to bark out orders to fellow owners. At their best, such companies eliminate the sense of "us" and "them" that pervades traditional companies—they become "us" companies in a way that is almost palpable. Again, however, none of this happens automatically. Companies must find ways to communicate the message that this workplace is different and that the role of employees and managers is not what it would be at a conventional business.

One technique for establishing a culture of ownership is simply to share large amounts of information about the business and its operations, including much of the financial data to which investor owners are traditionally privy and that senior managers use to run the business. Nearly all of the smaller companies we studied hold monthly all-hands meetings to review key financial figures and other issues of concern. Nearly all publish the numbers in newsletters or reports to their employees. SAIC conducts quarterly Webcasts, available to every employee, in which the CEO and CFO report on and analyze the company's financials, in much the same way that executives of publicly traded companies conduct quarterly conference calls with analysts and large investors. Note, however, that simply sharing consolidated financials at the corporate level once a quarter, in the manner of public companies, is not sufficient. What's important is that employees see the operational financials—plant, office, or store-level—that managers use to make decisions.

Conventional companies can assume that their principal owners don't need any instruction in matters like how to read a financial statement. Equity companies can't. So many devote substantial resources to training in business literacy. At Green Mountain Coffee Roasters, for instance—a six-hundred-person publicly traded company headquartered in Waterbury, Vermont—employees organized and taught a seven-and-a-half-hour course, spread out over three sessions, that instructed people in the basics of the company's business ("tree to cup") and financials. "By design, the classes were cross-functional," says Roger Garufi, a machine operator who was one of the course designers and instructors. "You'd be rubbing elbows with people from the senior leadership team or the roasters. Everyone in the classroom was in a different department, which was really nice."

A second technique is simplicity itself: before making decisions, managers ask employees what they think. One company—Atlas Container Corporation, a box-manufacturing business with several plants in the eastern United States—went so far as to ask shop-floor employees to choose between competing suppliers of a $1 million corrugating machine; when the employees selected an American-made model, the company's top executives agreed to the decision even though they favored an Italian machine.[4] YSI, a manufacturer of precision sensor measurement instruments with headquarters in Yellow Springs, Ohio, and thirteen other locations around the world, holds regular company meetings to discuss issues. Anytime YSI introduces something new, says chief executive Rick Omlor—a policy, a process, whatever—"we ask how people think about that, how they feel about it. As carefully as you might think about all the aspects of a new policy or plan, there will be two or three that you never [anticipated]. You just don't know what you don't know." Employee concerns, he adds, frequently lead to changes. "Every time we have done that, we have modified the plan or the process . . . It's not about people voting on everything and making every decision. But on big decisions that affect the whole company, at least let them participate in the discussions." At a growing number of companies, moreover, management simply entrusts employees to make decisions on their own. Teams at W. L. Gore & Associates and at many other businesses have considerable authority to run their own part of the workplace, including setting their own work schedules. Individual employees at Southwest Airlines and at many other businesses are allowed to make decisions on the spot, in the best interests of the customer, without asking a supervisor. We'll see more examples of this sort of self-management in chapter 6.

Equity companies have also developed a host of other techniques, at once symbolic and substantive, for breaking down hierarchy. Like Stone, for example, Scot Forge did away with time clocks and now describes itself as having an "all-salaried workforce." The phrase isn't strictly accurate—federal law requires nonsupervisory employees to be paid by the hour, because they must be paid overtime after forty hours a week—but it captures something important, which is that hourly employees are trusted partners and won't be docked if they have to run out to a doctor's appointment. The companies are also much more likely to implement the host of "participatory management" techniques that have become conventional wisdom (if not conventional practice) about how companies should be run. These include work cells, self-managing teams, cross-functional teams, open-book management, job enlargement, devolution of authority to lower levels, and other approaches to structuring—not just encouraging—employee involvement in workplace decisions.

Some of the cultural changes have a direct impact on people's careers and livelihoods. Equity companies make a point of cross-training people, encouraging career development, and promoting from within. They also take a different attitude toward layoffs, the threat of which has become the bane of nearly every employee's existence in today's turbulent economy. They may let people go in a pinch; no company that expects to survive can swear it will always maintain employment. But layoffs are a last resort, not a first. In 2003, Cindy Turcot, chief operating officer of Gardener's Supply, a catalog retailer in Burlington, Vermont, reflected on her company's situation:

> And this year again, we had a soft time, so I said, "These are the steps before we do a layoff. First, there will be no new positions. Then a pay freeze. Then pay cuts. Only then would we do lay-offs. So there are three steps before we do layoffs, and I will tell you every week if we have gone beyond step 1."
>
> I don't want people to go to fear. When they're in fear, when they think they're going to lose their job, I don't want that. So that's the goal: let people know where they are. Then they can go to the place of "What can I do?"

In fact, Turcot reports, the "What can I do?" mentality in this case was startlingly productive: Gardener's realized some $400,000 in savings over the course of the year, thanks to employee ideas. That made a big difference to the $60 million company's bottom line. "Even though sales are down," said Turcot, "we are going to hit our budget target for profitability. I attribute a lot of that to what employees are doing."

Business Discipline

All profitable companies make money by assembling a variety of components. They bring together capital equipment, money, and warm bodies, and they apply a series of business skills, such as production or service-delivery expertise, sales and marketing, and financial management. Exemplary companies are successful mostly because they learn to do things with some of these components that their competitors can't. They focus on one or more business disciplines and turn themselves into world-class practitioners. Thus no competitor has yet been able to match Intel's ability to produce and market leading-edge computer chips, or Wal-Mart Stores' ability to keep prices low.

At successful equity companies, employees both learn and drive the business disciplines that help their company do well. This is one key theme of the book you are holding. In the past, notions such as employee involvement and employee participation have been less than rigorously supported. They have been based on no more than a loose belief that it is good for companies, as well as good for people, to have employees a little more concerned with the day-to-day operations of the business. An explicit connection between that involvement and business performance has been lacking. When employees understand their companies' key business disciplines, however—when they understand both how to contribute to improving performance and how to measure the results of their efforts—the connection is clear. There is a line of sight from job to business performance, from engagement to results.

Not surprisingly, that connection is easiest to see in small companies, although the equity model can work just as well in large ones as in small ones. Consider the story of Jackson's Hardware, a sixty-seven-person, 100 percent employee-owned company in San Rafael, California.

Like Stone Construction Equipment, Jackson's is the kind of business most people think has vanished. It is an old-fashioned, single-store hardware and home-goods retailer that has survived and prospered right under the nose of big national chains. "We have a Home Depot located about a mile and a half from our store," said company president and general manager Bill Loskutoff. "We have an Orchard Supply—it's owned by Sears—about a half mile away." Loskutoff ticked off several other larger competitors—lumber yards, contractors' supply chains, a regional home-improvement center known as Yardbirds—and reported a curious fact. "When Orchard Supply came to town, our business increased. When Home Depot came to town, our business increased." Asked why, he shrugged. "People who were not customers of ours, maybe they had gone to various places and were dissatisfied. They thought they would find their ultimate hardware store at Home Depot, but they got there and found out it wasn't. They just kind of migrated over to us, and our business kept growing."

Jackson's competitive advantage lies in friendly and knowledgeable customer service, the kind often missing from big chain stores. It is set up to deliver precisely that. There are no cashiers: associates are expected to take customers through an entire transaction and to make sure they have everything they need. Managers and supervisors wear walkie-talkies on their belt so they can call in experts from another department if they can't personally answer a customer's question. Associates typically move from one department to another over time so that they can build their own stock of knowledge. (The average tenure at Jackson's in 2004 was roughly ten years.) The importance of customer service is drilled into every associate's head. "At larger companies, people don't seem to care as much," says Mark Helm, a warehouse supervisor who worked at Home Depot before coming to Jackson's. "The people here are more concerned, making sure they follow through with their customers. And if they don't, they have to answer for it. Don't leave the customer with bad service. Give good service. We're not going to differentiate ourselves [otherwise]."

From a financial perspective, however, what matters to Jackson's associates is weekly and monthly sales. The sales number is a gauge of how well they are serving their customers. It is also the store's key metric of business performance. Jackson's associates know that their colleagues can source the store's wares effectively and price them appropriately. So if sales are healthy, the bottom line will be healthy as well, and the company will prosper. Accordingly, people throughout the organization worry about sales levels the same way company founder H. C. Jackson must once have done, when he was the sole owner. The monthly sales goal and month-to-date figures are chalked up on a whiteboard in the lunchroom. A dip in sales is the occasion for quick action. In late 2003, for instance, associates noticed sales were a little sluggish, and someone proposed a special holiday sale. This is how one group remembered it a few months later:

Steve Graham, showroom manager: We were watching the monthly goals. We are on a fiscal year, July 1 to June 30, and we're a construction-oriented company—so the winter can be kind of dreary! It was a point where we were almost halfway through our year; we were doing OK, but we could really see that we could get up and over, hit our goals, or we could fall apart. It could definitely have gone either way. And from that, we started looking at, let's do everything—what can we do? Let's do everything we can to push this hard and get over the top and stay there.

Carolyn Emge, accounts-payable clerk: We were saying, what can we do? And everyone was throwing in ideas. [One idea was the special sale.] We had the monthly meeting and suggested to the other associates that without them we can't do the sale.

Robert Akins, service supervisor: And everybody came together. Everybody went in to decorate the store, work extra. And the buying team did a really great job by getting bonus [deals] with our vendors. So everybody did their part. Nobody was complaining about having to work overtime. It was just one big team effort.

Carolyn Emge: And we had a goal—wasn't it $100,000 in one day?—we had a goal that we were trying to meet, and it got fun during the last two hours. "Are we going to make it?" And we did!

Employees at other equity companies learn to focus on other metrics, depending on the key business disciplines. The metrics may be numbers right off the budget, or indeed right off the income statement (gross margin, cost of goods sold, net profit). Or they may be operational variables that directly affect the company's financial performance. Stone Construction Equipment's lean manufacturing system, for example, by itself boosts efficiency and lowers costs, when compared with traditional manufacturing. But employees' tracking and monitoring make the lean system even more efficient than it otherwise would be. The key number shop-floor employees watch is labor variance, meaning the difference between actual and budgeted labor content on any one product. Teams set labor variance goals. They track their performance day in and day out. Any time they beat their goal—symbols again—managers cook and serve the employees an elaborate meal. "I imagine [the mixer cell] will have steak, shrimp, and lobster on Friday," said Dick Nisbet one day in late 2003. "Their goal was a $3,500 labor variance for the month, and they came in at $4,700." Thus does Stone make itself a little bit more competitive, day in and day out, week after week and month after month.

So that is the equity model: stock ownership, a culture that enables people to feel and think like owners, and a shared commitment to key business disciplines. As we noted, we'll look in detail at the three elements in chapters 5, 6, and 7, one element per chapter. We'll dissect each one; we'll show how different companies put the basic notions into practice; and we'll draw out the lessons for companies that want to embark on this high-performance journey. But first we want to take a little detour into history. People familiar with management theory will recognize that our model has two ancestors: employee ownership, on the one hand, and what has been called participative (or participatory) management, on the other. The combination of the two makes for a particularly powerful change in employees' attitudes and actions, hence for a dramatic improvement in business performance. Curiously, however, these two strands have very different pasts. Despite some overlap, reformers and management innovators have typically focused on one or the other of the two goals, not on both at once. That led to some dead ends and disasters, such as what happened only a few years ago at United Airlines. If it's true that those who don't remember the past are condemned to repeat it, we should review these two disparate ideas carefully so that nobody again tries to separate them.

Part Two
ORIGINS

3

Louis Kelso and the Invention of Employee Ownership

"All truth passes through three stages," wrote the nineteenth-century philosopher Arthur Schopenhauer. "First, it is ridiculed. Second, it is violently opposed. Third, it is accepted as being self-evident." The idea that employees should own a good part of the company they work for was indeed both ridiculed and opposed before it became the quasi-mainstream notion that it is today. But it didn't proceed smoothly through Schopenhauer's stages. It has regularly cropped up and faded away. It has undergone periodic reinvention. Today's most common form—the ESOP—owes its existence not to any deep historical roots but to a small band of devotees who rallied around the ideas of an iconoclastic lawyer and self-taught social theorist named Louis Kelso. Thanks to their efforts, the ESOP is now well ensconced in the United States, both in policy and in practice. Even so—and true to the on-again, off-again history of the concept—it is by no means clear that the ESOP will be the most common form of employee ownership in the decades to come.

Louis Orth Kelso was an American original, the kind of grand contradictory character who crops up repeatedly in the history of the United States. Born poor, he made good. A successful lawyer and investment banker, he sought to transform the economic system that had been so rewarding to him. His several books are by turns inspiring, illuminating, impossibly grandiose, and utterly impenetrable. The economic world view he espoused attracted that band of devotees and generated a good deal of attention from pundits and politicians, yet was ignored or dismissed—indeed, ridiculed—by conventional economists. A charming, witty, persuasive man, he was also single-minded and opinionated. He suffered fools poorly—and "anybody who disagreed with him was by definition a fool," as one erstwhile colleague remembers. A 1970 article in *The Nation* by the journalist Robert Sherrill, though generally admiring, was headlined "Louis Kelso: Nut or Newton?" Like Sherrill, much of the world didn't quite know what to make of him.

As with many minor luminaries, what we know of Kelso's early life was what he himself told us. He was born on December 4, 1913, in Denver. His grandparents on both sides were of pioneer stock, but his father, a musician, was not of a practical turn of mind, and it often fell to his mother to support the family with the little grocery store she managed. (As best she could: "The railroad tracks ran alongside the store and the hobos dropped off at night and robbed the place too regularly to permit profit," wrote Sherrill, presumably reporting Kelso's recollections.)[1] Kelso was going on sixteen when the stock market crashed in October 1929, and he came to adulthood in the heart of the Great Depression. Bright and inquisitive, he wondered how on earth this catastrophe could be happening. Why were factories running at half speed, their unused machinery rusting?

> Why were millions of threadbare and ragged people foraging
> in garbage cans or standing in soup lines, when farmers could
> grow mountains of food and fiber on land now lying idle and
> manufacturers were as eager and able to make clothing and
> every other useful thing as storekeepers were to sell them? Why
> did growers saturate entire orchards of sweet ripe oranges with
> gasoline before throwing them into rivers to float past starving
> children? Why did trains meant to carry people rattle along
> with coaches almost empty, while freight trains were loaded
> down with homeless, jobless vagrants?[2]

His elders weren't much help: "They took it for granted that a capitalist economy would sooner or later collapse." President Hoover counseled patience, reminding the nation that the country had been through fifteen major depressions in the last century. Kelso was like an ambitious young scientist who learns that the authorities have given up on the single most important problem in his field. "Brash young man" that he was, he recalled, he decided he would figure out the answer.

So Kelso read, worked, and put himself through school. Landing a scholarship to the University of Colorado, he presented himself to the chairman of the economics department and said that he planned to study the causes of the Depression and what could be done about it. It was a touchy subject—economists didn't really know what was responsible for the Depression—and the chairman didn't take kindly to the cheeky fellow who figured he already had the inkling of a solution. ("He said, 'You're just the type of young man we don't want,'" recounts Kelso's widow, Patricia Hetter Kelso. "'You are a troublemaker.' So he kicked him out.") Instead of economics Kelso studied business and finance, earned a law degree, and began practicing. When war broke out, he enlisted in the navy and was commissioned as an officer in naval intelligence. "He was trained for a secret mission behind Japanese lines," writes Stuart M. Speiser, a lawyer-turned-author who is as close to a biographer of Kelso as we have, ". . . but he was shipped to the Panama Canal Zone and put in charge of processing counterespionage information from Latin America."[3] That undemanding job gave him the opportunity to produce a book manuscript, which he titled *The Fallacy of Full Employment*.

But when the war was over, Kelso decided against trying to get his new book published. He needed to earn a living. Maybe he was even a little uncertain as to whether he was on the right track. "I said to myself, 'Louis, you'd better settle down and practice law, which is what you're trained to do, and let the country recover from the war,'" he remembered later. "'Stick your manuscript in the closet, and if after 25 years you still think the thesis is valid, dig it out, update it, and publish it.'"[4] The "closet" was a bank vault, and there the manuscript stayed until 1955, when Kelso happened to get into a discussion with the philosopher Mortimer Adler.

That year, Kelso had been attending a series of lectures by Adler on Great Books. Great Books was a popular reading program that Adler had helped to develop and that had made his name about as close to a

household word as most philosophy professors ever get. Now, invited to
a weekend party by a mutual friend, the two men were arguing about
what they called the "theory of capitalism." Kelso charged Adler with ig-
norance of the theory. Adler suggested there was no such theory and
that he of all people ought to know. Kelso responded that Adler may
have thought he had read everything in the field, but he hadn't—the
manuscript in his closet, for example. Irritated—and worried that this
mouthy amateur would now present him with a huge dog-eared manuscript—Adler asked for the "five-minute version" of Kelso's ideas.
Kelso began expounding. When he had finished (again, by Kelso's account), Adler "jumped about 12 feet off the ground. 'There's no justice!'
he said. 'I've spent 22 years studying this subject, and you stumble
across the answer with no effort at all.'" In just a couple of years, the two
men had written a book they titled *The Capitalist Manifesto*, based
partly on Kelso's unpublished manuscript. They sent it off to four pub-
lishers. All accepted it; Random House published it in 1958. Thanks in
part to Adler's name, the book promptly made the best-seller list—
though the "academic economics establishment," as Speiser notes,
"practically ignored it."[5]

To read this modest-sized volume today—and not many people do,
since it is long out of print—is to step back into another era. That sense
of time warp stems partly from the book's cold war–inspired title and
language, and partly from its 1950s-style technological innocence ("It
seems certain that atomic energy will be the basic source of industrial
power for the production of wealth in the future").[6] It also stems from
the presentation itself. *The Capitalist Manifesto*'s arguments are abstract and almost startlingly dry ("Concretely stated, if A, B, C and D
are four persons or families in a society having only four independent
participants in the production of wealth; and if, through the use of the
productive property they own, A, B and C contribute to the total
wealth produced in the ratio 3, 2, 1, then the distributive shares they
should receive, according to their just deserts, should also be in the
ratio of 3, 2, 1 . . .").[7] Its proposals are laid out in mind-numbing detail
("Effective security flotation procedures during the transition period
may require the establishment of preferential opportunities for investment by households whose aggregate capital interests are subviable").[8]

A cynic might suggest that not everyone who bought the book actually plowed his or her way through it.

But the reviews were favorable, and there was a powerfully simple idea lurking amidst the verbiage. It was an idea that defined the book's appeal and that would eventually make Kelso into a nationally known figure.

In the 1950s, Americans were worried not only about the Russians but about being thrown out of a job. Unemployment wasn't unusually high, to be sure. But the nation's economic future seemed uncertain. Automation was making its way into industry. Economists and others were arguing that machines would eventually take over nearly all manual work. What were people to do? The Depression was fresh in every middle-aged adult's memory; equally dismal times might lie ahead. But wait—here was this smart guy Adler (and somebody named Kelso) with a solution! Yes, these authors said, the pace of automation was likely to increase. But no one should fear it, because it held the potential of releasing everybody from mind-numbing manual work. The key was to break the link between a person's income and survival on the one hand and his or her job on the other. *No one should have to live on labor income alone.* If more people enjoyed what the rich already enjoyed, namely ownership of capital and the income that flowed from that ownership, they would get along just fine. If you have enough stock, after all, you don't worry about unemployment. And if everyone had an income regardless of whether or not they were working, they could continue to buy things. The economy would be that much less likely to collapse.

Could the idea be implemented? Sure, said the authors. The rules governing ownership and capital accumulation are just social inventions. Social inventions can be changed. If we really want a just, democratic society—not to mention an economy that isn't prone to depression—we can create mechanisms by which ordinary people can build up capital and eventually live off it. We can figure out policies that enable the process. We can write tax laws that facilitate it. Indeed, we can begin right now, with the "transitional programs" that the authors spelled out in so much detail. The programs' objective was simple, they said: it "should be to maintain a steady decrease in the proportion of households that are entirely dependent on wages and a steady increase in the number that are able to live on capital earnings."[9]

That, so it seemed, was an idea that anybody could get behind. Forget socialism, Adler and Kelso were arguing. Let's turn everybody into capitalists.

CO-OPS AND CORPORATE LEADERS

Kelso, of course, was not the first to come up with the notion that workers should make themselves—or be made into—owners.[10] Various people in both labor and management had been espousing it for many years, albeit in different forms.

Ever since the early nineteenth century, for example, workers in a particular trade or business would occasionally band together to start a company. But they would often organize it as a cooperative rather than as a corporation. The co-op's employees would thus share ownership and control, typically on a one-person, one-vote basis. Flannel weavers in Rochdale, England, tried twice in the 1830s to establish a cooperative textile business but failed; finally, in 1844, a group that included weavers and men from other trades established a cooperatively owned store that sold foodstuffs, tea, and tobacco. The Rochdale Society of Equitable Pioneers, widely recognized as the founding fathers of co-ops, developed a set of rules and procedures that have influenced both producer and consumer cooperatives ever since. In the United States, labor organizations such as the Knights of Labor sponsored producer co-ops, and skilled workers often set them up on their own. "Between 1866 and 1876 shoeworkers operated at least 40 [cooperative] factories and moulders at least 36 foundries," writes one historian:

> . . . In addition, bakers, coach-makers, collar makers, shipwrights, nailers, ship-carpenters and caulkers, glassblowers, hatters, boiler-makers, plumbers, and iron rollers organized cooperative workshops. A total of at least 500 cooperative workshops and factories opened for business in the twenty-five years following the Civil War. Two hundred and ninety of these producer establishments commenced business between 1884 and 1888 [alone] . . . In 1885, fifteen percent of the 1228 shoe

workers of Stoneham [Massachusetts] worked in co-operative shoe factories.[11]

The cooperative movement—for a movement it was, however disjointed—fared differently in different countries. Co-ops in Britain proliferated for a time, numbering about two thousand by the year 1900, but most later died out.[12] Co-ops in Spain and Italy both proliferated and flourished throughout the twentieth century, right down to the present day. The giant Mondragón cooperative enterprises, in the Basque region of Spain, have grown steadily since the founding of a co-op factory to make oil stoves and heaters in 1956:

> By the end of the [twentieth] century the Mondragón Cooperative Corporation was one of the largest corporations in Spain; it is the country's largest supplier of domestic appliances and machine tools, and an important supplier of car parts, employing twenty-six thousand people in a hundred industrial, financial, and retail companies. Eighty of these businesses are cooperative.
>
> Woven into this network of businesses are worker education and training centers, universities, research centers, and service cooperatives. The cooperatives are worker-owned and democratically managed. Each worker has the right to vote colleagues onto a general assembly that elects the board. No one in the company earns more than six times the salary of the lowest paid worker. Typically, when a company grows to more than five hundred employees, the parent finances another start-up company to ensure that each unit remains relatively small and manageable.[13]

Except in agriculture, U.S. producer co-ops mostly faded away. But one could always find a handful of small cooperative enterprises scattered around the country, and medium-scale co-ops continued to survive well into the second half of the twentieth century in two distinct market niches. In the 1940s, workers in several plywood mills in the Pacific Northwest organized themselves into co-ops and bought out their employers, who were about to shut the mills down. Some of the cooperative mills prospered for three decades or more, and when finally sold, brought each of their worker-owners a six-figure return. In the 1920s, groups of Italian immigrants set up cooperatively owned refuse collection companies in the San Francisco area. The scavengers, as they were collectively known, dominated the industry in that region and functioned as successful co-ops for several decades. "It was not to be expected," declared the bylaws of the Sunset Scavenger Company, "that a hired scavenger would work as well as and as willingly as one who is a shareholder."[14] The legacy of this phenomenon is visible today: Sunset is now part of giant Norcal Waste Systems, which is 100 percent employee owned through an ESOP.

Historically, the idea that workers should be owners drew as much (or more) support from American corporate leaders as from labor. In both cases it was a minority view, but on the management side the idea attracted the backing of powerful figures and for a while seemed the likely next step in the evolution of capitalism. Leland Stanford, the railroad magnate who founded Stanford University and became a U.S. senator, introduced a bill in 1886 to encourage employee ownership. "What I believe," he explained in an 1887 interview, "is, the time has come when the laboring men can perform for themselves the office of becoming their own employers."[15] Harvard president Charles W. Eliot wrote an article supporting employee ownership and "cooperative management." John D. Rockefeller Jr. formed a commission in 1919 that urged companies to sell stock to employees at a discount.

By then, some big companies were already doing just that. The list included Procter & Gamble, Illinois Central Railroad, Pittsburgh Coal Company, the National Biscuit Company, the First National Bank of Chicago, and E. I. du Pont de Nemours and Company. But the pace picked up after 1919. Kodak founder George Eastman offered more than 8 percent of the company's stock to employees at a steep discount. The various Standard Oil companies, following the Rockefeller commission's recommendations, sold their employees discounted stock. By the late 1920s, employees owned roughly 6 percent of AT&T, 7 percent of Bethlehem Steel, and 12 percent of Procter & Gamble.[16] General Electric offered discounted shares to its employees, to be paid for in installments, beginning in 1920. In 1927, GE chairman Owen D. Young gave a speech to a Harvard Business School audience, saying:

I hope the day may come when these great business organizations will truly belong to the men who are giving their lives and their efforts to them, I care not in what capacity . . . Then, in a word, men will be as free in cooperative undertakings and subject only to the same limitations and chances as men in individual businesses. Then we shall have no hired men.

The speech was reprinted verbatim in the *New York Times*.[17]

To be sure, there were problems with the early plans, and skeptics abounded. GE found that many employees had quickly sold their stock, often to con artists.[18] (The company replaced its initial stock plan with a plan offering GE bonds; the bonds paid a nominal 6 percent a year, but 8 percent if the employee held them and remained on the payroll.) The influential labor economist Sumner Slichter, writing in 1929, opined that employee stock ownership was "among the least significant of the [nation's] new labor policies," largely because owning a few shares of stock didn't do much to change the employee's perspective on the company or his job.[19] Young found that his seemingly historic speech at Harvard generated only a little interest: "By and large," observe his biographers, "the economists and pundits paid it little mind."[20] At any rate, the positives and negatives were soon made moot. As the tidal wave of the Great Depression washed over the country, it swept away any notion that workers should be owners. Share prices were plummeting. Jobs were evaporating. Employees began to feel that they had been played for suckers with all the talk about ownership and cooperation. Desperate to preserve jobs and wages, those who stayed on company payrolls joined unions in droves—and no union at the time was proposing any form of employee ownership.

Here, too, some of the dynamics are most clearly visible in smaller companies, and the historian Robert Bussel has provided a telling case study. The Columbia Conserve Company, located in Indianapolis, had been bought in 1903 by one William Hapgood. A thirty-one-year-old scion of a leading Chicago family, son of a progressive businessman and brother of two muckraking journalists, Hapgood subscribed to the idea that industrialization had "hurt human beings" and that labor and capital should cooperate.[21] Columbia Conserve when he bought it was a struggling producer of canned soups employing about thirty people.

So Hapgood's first job was to put the company on its financial feet, which took several years. But by the 1920s it was generating steady profits and employing upwards of one hundred full-time people, along with many seasonal workers. Now he felt he could experiment with some of his ideas about industrial cooperation. He put every full-timer on salary. He began offering medical, dental, and eye care to everybody, and generous pensions to the company's few retirees. He created an elected council to govern company operations, including decisions about wages and hours. He also created a trust, funded by company profits, to buy Columbia Conserve's stock on behalf of its employees. By 1930 the employees as a group had become majority owners. Like many ESOP companies today, Columbia Conserve advertised its ownership structure along with its products: it was "the only soup in the world made on the principle—100% Food Quality in the can, 100% Human Equality in the plant." Hapgood gave many speeches about the company, and the press began writing up the experiment as the "business without a boss."

But the 1930s were difficult and fractious years for Columbia Conserve. Demand plunged as the Depression deepened. Profits vanished. Hoping to preserve their benefits, employees agreed to a series of pay cuts. But pensions and health insurance were scaled back anyway. Upset with the company's difficulties, a dissident group of salesmen challenged Hapgood's still-dominant role in the governing council. Hapgood fought with them for a while and then fired them. Over time, he asserted ever-greater control. In 1942, workers voted to join a union affiliated with the American Federation of Labor and went on strike for five days. Hapgood said he would recognize the union only if workers renounced their ownership stake. The War Labor Board intervened. Finally, all parties agreed that the experiment would come to an end. The stock owned by the workers as a group would be distributed to individuals, to do with it whatever they liked. Hapgood would once again be the largest single shareholder and would run the business. "The Columbia Conserve experiment in industrial democracy is at an end," stated a 1943 report by the War Labor Board. "The Company is to revert to the condition of the ordinary American corporation." The declaration could serve as an epitaph for all the experimentation in worker ownership that had seemed so promising in the 1920s.

KELSO'S PLANS AND PROGRAMS

Kelso was doubtless aware of all that history. He had read widely, and *The Capitalist Manifesto* makes occasional reference to historical precedent. But he had different objectives from his employee-ownership forebears. Where they were concerned primarily with "the labor question"—how workers in any one company should share in the wealth they helped create, and how labor and management could work together in harmony, rather than winding up at each other's throats—he was concerned with broad social issues. Capitalism in Kelso's view had always been marked by a maldistribution of income. The rich got richer because they enjoyed the fruits of capital ownership. The not-rich struggled to get along, because they lived only on the fruits of their labor. With automation, the return to capital could only increase, and workers could lose what little income they had. Governmental attempts to redistribute income through social programs were ineffectual. The only solution was to broaden the base of capital ownership.

As to how that might be possible, Kelso's brilliant insight was to see that individual savings alone would never be sufficient—especially if, as he predicted, real wages began to stagnate. Few wage earners could ever hope to accumulate enough capital to replace their labor income just by stashing a little away each year. That was the trouble with the plans of the 1920s: they expected workers to buy stock, albeit at a discount, a little at a time, through payroll deductions. Kelso had another idea. Look at what happens, he suggested, when a company owner wants to expand his business. The owner borrows money, buys physical capital such as machinery or buildings, and pays off the loan with the profits that the new capital generates. Every year U.S. businesses added billions of dollars' worth of new physical capital. Suppose the laws were changed, suggested Kelso, so that people with no ownership got a chance to buy shares of stock representing that new capital. They could borrow the money to buy the shares and *pay the loan off over time with the dividends from the stock.* To ensure that dividends would be sufficient for this purpose, Kelso advocated a law requiring corporations to pay out all their earnings as dividends and to raise new capital through debt (which in turn could be funded by an ESOP).

Presto—the rich would still get to keep what they had, but now the not-rich would be able to accumulate capital of their own as the economy grew. And nobody would be getting a handout, because all the stock would be paid for through future earnings.

In his books, Kelso spelled out only some of the practical details as to how all this could be accomplished. He left many others to be worked out in the future. But he was very much proposing a broad-based governmental initiative, open to all needy citizens, and very much *not* proposing shared ownership at the company level, which by definition would be open only to that company's employees. The ESOP—mentioned only briefly in *The Capitalist Manifesto* and not at all in Kelso and Adler's next book, *The New Capitalists*—was at first a bit player on Kelso's grand stage. Oddly, it wound up as the star of his show and was arguably his greatest legacy.

How that happened reflects one more contradiction in Kelso's multifaceted character. A determined visionary and big-picture thinker, he was at the same time a practical lawyer and an opportunistic political operator who never let his theories get in the way of what could be done right now. In 1955, for example, he was a junior partner in a San Francisco law firm. One of the firm's clients was part owner of a company called Peninsula Newspapers, Inc. (PNI), which published several small papers. Kelso learned that this client and the other owners of PNI wanted to sell the company to its employees. He also learned that the employees liked the idea and were working hard to make it happen. A man named Gene Bishop, who coincidentally had been Kelso's commanding officer in the navy, was now second-in-command at PNI and was spearheading the effort on the employees' behalf. The parties had engaged Crocker Bank to scrutinize the relevant finances. Could Bishop and his colleagues put together the capital they needed to buy the paper through savings, payroll deductions, second mortgages, investments from relatives, and so on?

Alas, the bank's conclusion was negative. There just wasn't enough money to be found. If the employees borrowed what they needed, they could afford to pay only the interest, not the principal. "When Gene Bishop passed my office that day," Kelso remembered, "I said to him, 'Hey, Gene, are you a newspaper owner now?' He said no and told me the story. I said, 'Gene, I think it's very possible you were given bad advice.' . . . He said, 'Listen, this is a life-and-death matter for me. I'm not going to stay with this newspaper if it's going to be sold to Hearst or some other chain. I like it the way it is.'" So Kelso said he would look at the file and see what he could come up with. Next day he reported his conclusions to Bishop. "'Gene,' I said, 'this thing will fly like a birdie. You don't have to take anything out of your pockets or out of your paychecks. You don't have to mortgage your house. You don't have to do any of those things. Five or six years downstream, the employees will own the business free and clear. And the present owner will have his money and his interest.' Gene thought I was kidding, but I was not."[22]

The secret, of course, was for the buyers to pay for their ownership out of the company's future earnings. It is a familiar principle today, since it is the basis for most of the leveraged buyouts (LBOs) that have taken place in the last few decades. But in the mid-1950s it was an astonishing notion. Kelso set up profit-sharing trusts to borrow the money to buy the business from the retiring owners. Employees' individual accounts were credited with share ownership as the trusts paid off the loans. "Kelso's blueprint was a smashing success," reports Speiser. The newspaper company prospered. The trusts paid off the original owners even faster than Kelso had allowed for. By 1974 PNI's balance sheet showed shareholders' equity of more than $6 million.[23] When the employees did finally sell to another newspaper publisher, they realized a huge return on their minimal investments.

So Kelso spent the 1960s and early 1970s organizing more such buyouts. (They came to be known as Kelso Plans, a label he found distasteful.) He also continued with his contradictory life. He was a successful San Francisco lawyer and later an investment banker. He was a member of the best clubs, a director of several companies, a frequent attendee at the annual summertime Bohemian Grove retreats, known for attracting the cream of the (male) establishment. His habitual dress included a well-tailored suit and a blue bow tie with white polka dots. On the other hand, he was devoted to spreading what he was ever more frequently calling his "revolution." He wrote more books, collaborating now not with Adler but with his young research associate Patricia Hetter, whom he later would marry. He gave numberless speeches and wrote (again with Hetter) many articles. He whispered in the ears of powerful businessmen, believing he could persuade them to implement his notions. "His idea was to start the capitalist revolution through the business system," says Patricia Hetter Kelso. But the ears, however attentive to Kelso they might be at the moment, were seemingly deaf to what he was arguing for.

So Kelso decided to launch an attack on Washington, hoping there might be a way to line up political leaders behind his ideas. Granted, he had had only spotty success with this approach so far. Barry Goldwater, the Republican candidate for president in 1964, "listened politely" to Kelso at the Bohemian Grove that year, but deferred judgment on the ideas to his economic adviser, Milton Friedman. Like nearly all academic economists, right and left, Friedman thought Kelso was far more nut than Newton. Gerald Ford, then a congressman, got excited about Kelso's ideas and set up a meeting in 1965 with a Republican task force; later that year, Kelso spent several hours with Richard Nixon, who declared himself "no economist" but added, "politically I could sell this to the American people in six months."[24] Neither meeting led to anything. Undaunted, Kelso in 1968 set up a Washington-based organization he called the Institute for the Study of Economic Systems and hired an idealistic young attorney and civil rights activist named Norman Kurland to head it.

Kurland and Kelso put together a board for their institute, making a point to include representatives from the left (longshore union leader Harry Bridges, future D.C. mayor Marion Barry) and from the right (the chairman of Arthur Andersen, actress Shirley Temple Black). They set about raising money, though without much success. ("By 1970 Kelso could no longer pay me," remembers Kurland.) Kurland began casting about, both for receptive ears and for legislation that he could push in a Kelsonian direction. Senator Paul Fannin of Arizona was intrigued enough to sponsor Kurland's "wish list" legislation, dubbed the Accelerated Capital Formation Act, and invited Kelso to make a presentation to several members of the Senate Finance Committee. But the legislation went nowhere. In 1972, Kelso and Kurland testified on legislation to save the financially troubled railroad system in the eastern

United States, proposing that it should be owned by its employees. Senator Mark Hatfield of Oregon liked the idea, agreed to sponsor legislation to this effect, and was joined by four other senators. But it was still a rearguard action unlikely to garner much support.

At that point Kelso tried a different tack. He wanted more than anything else to get to Russell Long, the Louisiana senator who was chairman of the Finance Committee and one of the most powerful men anywhere in government. Long, he thought, not only might be receptive, he also was in a position where he could get something done. So Kelso began nosing around to see who might know him. Kelso's friend Henry McIntyre, a fund-raiser for Planned Parenthood, had an idea: his organization's national chairman, a Louisiana physician named Joe Beasley, might know Long. Sure enough, Beasley did. But he recommended that they approach Long by way of his legislative assistant, Wayne Thevenot.

Beasley called Thevenot—the name is pronounced TEV-uh-no— and sent him a copy of a 1968 Kelso and Hetter book called *Two-Factor Theory: The Economics of Reality*. (The original and much better title of the 1967 hardback edition had been *How to Turn Eighty Million Workers Into Capitalists on Borrowed Money*.) Then Beasley started calling. Had Thevenot read it? When he still hadn't, some months later, Beasley said he was flying to San Francisco and invited Thevenot to join him, at Beasley's expense. Thevenot agreed: "It was the last part of that proposal that caught my attention," he said later. He took the book with him to read on the plane. He didn't like it. "There was obviously something wrong with it. It was too damned easy," he told Speiser. But after two days of listening to Kelso's persuasive voice, he changed his mind and suddenly had all the passion of the newly converted. "I just became totally sold on the idea," he recalled. He went back to Washington to try to persuade his boss, Russell Long.[25]

Long was the son of Huey Long, the legendary Louisiana "Kingfish" who wanted to make every man a king. More than just Finance Committee chair, Russell was a brilliant politician in the mold of Lyndon Johnson, both well liked and well respected by senators on both sides of the aisle. What he supported tended to get passed. What he didn't support tended to get buried. As for his politics, Long wasn't the soak-the-rich radical his father had been—indeed, he was often perceived as just another southern Democrat whose prime concern was the health of the oil and gas industries—but he still had several populist bones in his body. So Kelso's ideas didn't require a hard sell from Thevenot. "I didn't have to go very far because Long started tracking on it right quick," remembered Thevenot. ". . . He said, 'I've got to meet this guy Kelso.'"[26]

On November 27, 1973, they met. Kurland had picked Kelso up at the airport the day before. On the way in, they had heard the well-known newscaster Eric Sevareid supporting Senator Hatfield's Kelso-like proposal for the railroads. It seemed a favorable omen. The next day, they went to the Senate, where Long was engaged in a debate on campaign reform, and waited in the gallery. At seven o'clock Long sent for his limousine. The four men—including Thevenot—went to the tony Montpelier Room in Washington's Madison Hotel for dinner.

Dinner lasted three or four hours. Kelso outlined his ideas. Long listened and then began to talk. He told anecdotes about Huey. He expounded notions of his own. His father had been a "Robin Hood" populist, he said. He himself wasn't a Robin Hood populist, but he liked the idea of more people becoming capitalists. Of course, he had questions and concerns. If everyone was an owner, would they be like the idle rich, never working? And if this was such a good idea, why hadn't it already gone further? Who was against it? Kelso's answers are lost to history. But they were evidently satisfactory, because a couple of hours into the conversation, Long's tone changed. "Louis, you've made your sale," Thevenot recalls him saying. "Now, what can I do to help you?" Kurland promptly interjected that they already had a bill, introduced by Senator Hatfield, to apply Kelso's ideas to the railroads. "I said, 'We need somebody with guts to take this and make it into law,'" remembers Kurland. "He looked at me and said, 'You bring me something tomorrow morning.'"

From that moment forward, Kelso's ideas were a live issue in Washington and would be written into a series of legislative initiatives over a period of many years. But there was a twist: what Long had fastened onto, ironically, was the idea that *workers in a company* should share ownership, through ESOPs, not that the government should somehow make ownership available to citizens in general. Speiser asked him why he focused on ESOPs rather than on the more general thrust of Kelso's writings. Long replied that ESOPs were a stepping stone, a device that "starts people thinking about the idea." Eventually, people would have to figure out how to redistribute *all* the new wealth that the nation created every year, but not right away. "He doesn't have the whole blueprint drawn up yet," observed Speiser, whose book appeared in 1977, "but he's going to keep on writing ESOP into every tax law in which he can find it. He's going to try to force corporations to broaden the ownership of new capital, even if he has to do it all by himself."[27]

THE ESOP SAGA

The history of ESOPs since that time reflects, in no small measure, Long's efforts to do exactly what Speiser predicted. He began by trying to get employee ownership into the Railroad Reorganization Act. But other senators were leery because the rail unions weren't on board, and Congress ended up deciding only to sponsor a study of the idea. Long then inserted provisions regarding ESOPs into the Employee Retirement Income Security Act (ERISA), the landmark legislation that has governed company-sponsored retirement accounts ever since its passage in 1974. This was a turning point. Until then, Kelso and his associates had been setting up legal entities known as stock bonus plans, which then borrowed money to buy stock from retiring owners. They argued that the law permitted this. But most lawyers disagreed, so Kelso found it difficult to sell his ideas to many companies. ERISA—which happened to be the bill that was moving through Congress and that Long felt he could use to make such transactions legal—finally put the government's imprimatur on Kelso's ideas. "Before ERISA passed, we were dealing with a much higher degree of skepticism," explains Ron Ludwig, an attorney who worked with Kelso at the time. "We had to show people and their lawyers that this was in fact legal. Once ERISA passed it became easier. They were still skeptical . . . but it was easier than dealing with no law at all." Of course, it was simply historical coincidence that ERISA was the first law governing ESOPs. It was the "tax train leaving the station at the time," as one expert puts it, and Long's expertise and inclination naturally pointed him in the direction of supporting ESOPs by writing them into tax law.

At any rate, ERISA was just the start. Over the next dozen years, Long was instrumental in passing numerous pieces of ESOP-related legislation. (Many would be amendments to ERISA, while others were amendments to the tax code.) He didn't have to do it all by himself, as Speiser had suggested he might; on the contrary, he was already inspiring a band of devotees who—if they hadn't done so already—were now deciding to commit their lives to furthering employee ownership. Kelso, Thevenot, and Kurland, the triumvirate that had started Long down this path, continued their efforts. So did Jack Curtis, a staff member of the Senate Finance Committee, and Kelso associate Ron Ludwig. One of the authors of this book (Corey Rosen) was a staffer for the Senate Small Business Committee at the time; a young academic named Joseph Blasi was working on the House side as an aide to a newly elected representative. "The House and Senate staffers started meeting for lunches," Blasi remembers, "and we started cooperating on bills and discussions. Out of those meetings came a lot of things . . . [including] a lot more obvious House support for Russell Long's initiatives in the Senate." When Jack Curtis went on to practice ESOP law, a lawyer named Jeff Gates, who had worked with Ludwig in San Francisco, took Curtis's place on the Finance Committee staff. Gates, who today is recognized as a leader in the field of employee ownership, liked to work on a dozen different possibilities at once. "I'd come up with fifteen ideas," he recalls. "He [Long] would go with ten of them into the Finance Committee, hope to get eight of them out of committee and maybe three out of conference. And the last time I looked, we had twenty-five separate pieces of federal legislation."

Today, much of that legislation has come and gone, amended beyond recognition or simply allowed to expire. The Tax Reduction Act of 1975, for example, created the Tax Credit Stock Ownership Plan, known as TRASOP, giving employers a 1 percent tax credit on certain capital investments if they contributed a corresponding amount of stock to an ESOP. In effect, the government was paying companies to print shares and give them to employees. The provision was popular with large companies, but it didn't in fact get much stock into employees' hands. In 1981 the Economic Recovery Tax Act phased out TRASOPs in favor of a new device known as the PAYSOP (payroll-based stock ownership plan), in which the government effectively *bought* a company's stock through tax credits and gave it to employees. That, too, was popular, but it expired at the end of 1986. Meanwhile, employee-

ownership provisions were inserted into various bits of special legislation. The Chrysler Loan Guarantee Act of 1979, for instance—otherwise known as the Chrysler bail-out—required Chrysler to create an
ESOP and provide it with 25 percent ownership of the company over
four years.[28] Meanwhile, too, large public companies that felt themselves vulnerable to hostile takeover realized that a large block of stock
held by "friendly" owners—their employees—might keep the corporate raiders at bay. ESOPs proliferated among large businesses for that
reason alone.

They also proliferated for a reason Kelso had never imagined. In
1979, when Corey Rosen was working for the Small Business Committee, a man named Ed Sanders came into the office. He owned a twenty-
employee plywood distributor in Alexandria, Virginia, called Allied
Plywood. He wanted to sell the business to those employees through an
ESOP, but he wasn't happy with one part of the deal. If another corporation bought his company and paid him in stock, he noted—John
Deere and others had made offers—he could defer capital gains tax on
the proceeds. But if he sold to the ESOP, he'd have to pay the taxes right
away. That didn't seem fair. He himself would sell to the ESOP anyway,
he said, but he thought that other company owners should get a better
deal if they did the same.

So Rosen drafted a bill allowing for deferral of capital gains taxes
for company owners who sold a certain percentage of their stock to an
ESOP. Long and his staff didn't think the provision was important.
Rosen's boss, the liberal senator Gaylord Nelson, feared it was too so-
cialistic. (Rosen reminded Sen. Nelson that Barry Goldwater, Russell
Long, and Orrin Hatch, a conservative from Utah, all backed employee ownership.) But another committee member, Donald Stewart,
a liberal senator from Alabama serving out the remains of a fill-in
two-year term (he was not reelected), did introduce the bill and got
Long, Nelson, and a bipartisan group of House and Senate members
to go along with it. And though it didn't pass right away, the provision
survived; in 1984, almost as an afterthought, it was tossed into a late-
night conference-committee agreement on a tax bill that contained a
number of ESOP amendments, including eliminating the PAYSOP. In
fact, Long made the requirements even more lenient than Rosen had
suggested. That provision—the deferral of taxes on the sale of private-

company stock to an ESOP—has been a key incentive for the creation of thousands of such plans.

So ESOPs spread, and the community of people interested in them grew in number and in influence. Kelso himself continued to lead the charge. He gave more speeches, wrote more books, and coauthored more articles. He was admiringly profiled on television by Mike Wallace on *60 Minutes* in 1975 and by Bill Moyers on *World of Ideas* in 1990. (The *60 Minutes* profile included scornful comments from the noted economist Paul Samuelson, who thereby seemed to be ridiculing just about the best idea to come down the pike in a long time.) A trade organization, the ESOP Association, came into existence. Rosen left the government and, with Karen Young, created the National Center for Employee Ownership (NCEO) as a center for research, information, and advocacy. To be sure, the spread of employee ownership provoked some opposition. Labor unions strongly disliked the idea at first, perhaps wondering whether workers who were also owners would really need a union. Some Reagan administration officials also wanted to get rid of ESOPs. Most people, of course, just ignored the whole thing—or if they knew about it, wrote it off as of marginal importance. It continued to grow, nevertheless. Over time, law firms, consulting firms, and business-valuation firms began to specialize in ESOP work. Banks learned how to do ESOP-related lending. Articles began to appear on companies that were owned by their workers; the companies themselves began mentioning their ownership in their ads. By 1990 well over ten thousand companies had ESOPs covering millions of employees, a constituency that Congress was loath to antagonize. To all appearances, employee ownership in this particular guise was here to stay.

But in fact there were three major sources of uncertainty about its future.

One reflected the fact that ESOPs were, by law, financial instruments. The plans were singled out for special treatment by the U.S. tax code. ESOP transactions were governed by rules determined by Congress, the Department of Labor, and the IRS. Many companies adopted them simply because they made financial sense for the owners. But it seemed at the time that a change in the tax code or the accounting rules could therefore jeopardize the plans' existence.

In Congress, for example, some sort of ESOP abuse would periodically come to light, and ESOP opponents would threaten to abolish the favorable tax treatment altogether. The employee-ownership community for the most part was diligent and effective in persuading Congress to maintain the tax breaks. The task was harder after Sen. Long retired in 1986, but by then the community was large enough and strong enough to wage successful political battles even without Long's commanding presence. The accounting profession was a different matter. In 1992 the American Institute of Certified Public Accountants (AICPA) set up new guidelines that changed the rules for leveraged ESOPs—that is, ESOPs that had borrowed money. Under the new rules, companies making contributions to ESOPs would report lower earnings than they had before. (Their actual cash flow would not change—only the earnings they reported under the rules of accounting.) Publicly traded companies, whose stock prices rise and fall with reported earnings, suddenly found ESOPs less attractive. If they wanted to give employees stock, they now were likely to channel it through 401(k) retirement plans rather than through an ESOP. Or else they used stock options.

Options themselves were a second source of uncertainty, because—for a while, at least—they seemed so much more popular than ESOPs. A few high-technology firms had pioneered the idea in the 1960s and 1970s of giving stock options to "key" employees.[29] That group typically included senior executives and experienced electronics engineers, who at the time were scarce. Options had a threefold appeal for the young tech companies that began using them. For one thing, they were a powerful form of incentive compensation. If the company survived, grew, and went public, its options holders could realize sums equivalent to several years' salary or more. For another, options (like ESOPs) were thought to encourage employees to think and act like owners. Tech start-ups typically expected their employees to work long hours, often for lower salaries than they could earn elsewhere; options gave them a long-term stake in the business's success and hence would encourage them to think more about long-term potential than short-term discomfort. Best of all, options were essentially free, or at least seemed free on the income statement. A company handing out a

$10,000 cash bonus had that much less cash in the bank, and it had to record the money as an expense on its income statement, thereby lowering any profits it might otherwise have had. A company handing out $10,000 in options (however they might be valued) wasn't spending any cash at all—and according to accounting rules, it didn't even have to record the options as an expense. (Of course, ultimately there would be a bill to pay when the options were exercised; companies at that point would have to buy back higher-priced shares and resell them to employees at lower prices, or else just print more shares, leading to downward pressure on share prices.)

At any rate, options spread like wildfire. Soon technology companies were handing them out not just to senior management and key engineers but to salespeople and middle managers; not much later, many were distributing them to everyone on the payroll. The more companies that did so, the more pressure there was for competitors to do likewise. Bit by bit, the use of options spread beyond high technology. Companies such as PepsiCo and Starbucks passed out options to most of their workforce out of philosophical commitment, believing that it would build a cooperative atmosphere and help them attract the best employees. Big pharmacy chains and some of the larger banks handed them out because—in the hothouse labor markets of the 1990s—they were having difficulty attracting and keeping *any* employees. Options eventually gained a kind of cachet, to the point where it was not unusual for any CEO in any industry to wake up one morning and announce that the company would give everybody one hundred options. In the 1990s, with the stock market constantly on the rise, it was like handing out candy.

But then, of course, a double-bladed ax fell. The stock market collapse left many, many options holders "under water" with little prospect of recovery anytime soon.[30] The market's bumpy, uneven recovery since its initial collapse left a lot of people apprehensive about options—who could say how much they might ever be worth, let alone when? Partly because of such concerns, Microsoft phased out its options program and replaced it with a so-called restricted stock program. (Restricted stock does not vest until certain conditions are met, such as the company's hitting certain targets or the employee's reaching a certain number of years of service.) A few other companies began to follow suit. Then, too, the accounting profession finally seemed about to decide that companies could no longer have a free ride when it came to issuing options: unless Congress passes legislation to the contrary (which at this writing seems unlikely), beginning in mid-2005 (for public companies) or in 2006 (for closely held companies), any company issuing options will have to value them according to set formulas and then deduct the amount from its reported earnings ("expense" them). As this book goes to press, no one knows exactly what the effect of the new rule will be. Data compiled by the NCEO indicates that the stock market's likely reaction to options expensing will be a big yawn.[31] If that's the case, companies are likely to make decisions about equity compensation based on more essential economic decisions, such as how the distribution of ownership in a company affects performance.

THE UNANSWERED QUESTION

And then there was the biggest question of all, which was why anyone should care about ESOPs, options, or all the other vagaries and uncertainties of employee ownership.

What, after all, was the purpose of making workers into owners? Kelso was concerned with creating a fairer distribution of wealth, particularly since automation seemed likely to throw people out of work. But neither automation nor anything else other than cyclical downturns has increased the rate of unemployment since Kelso's day. Indeed, in the 1980s and 1990s, more people were holding down jobs than ever before. Moreover—quite unlike Kelso's original idea—the ESOPs that became the practical incarnation of his vision were specifically tied to employment. So were options. The result was that a lucky group of workers had both good jobs *and* capital ownership, while the majority of workers still had only a job. ESOPs and options might be creating a more equitable distribution of the wealth created by any one company, but they weren't making much of a dent in the overall economic system.

That stark fact brought employee ownership advocates back to the "labor question." If ESOPs or options *really* helped people think and act like owners—if employees took a more collaborative approach to their work, and if they somehow behaved differently on the job—then

maybe that was the justification for ownership. Ownership would create labor peace. It would improve productivity and the nation's international competitiveness. Advocates had always assumed that ownership
would have these beneficial effects, but they didn't know for sure. Did
a modest amount of company stock tucked away in a retirement account alter how an employee viewed his or her job? And what about
options? Did they make a real difference—or were they, as one ESOP
advocate liked to grouse, "the crack cocaine of employee ownership,"
giving the employee a brief high when they were cashed in but creating
no long-term difference in outlook?

Equally puzzling, the press periodically reported stories of employee-
owned companies that crashed and burned. A company called South
Bend Lathe, for example, was bought out by its employees (with Kelso's
and Kurland's help) way back in 1975. Five years later the employees
went out on strike, seemingly against themselves. So it was at various
other employee-owned companies: every now and then, one would
wind up on the rocks, often plagued by continuing labor-management
conflict. In the 1990s, two of United Airlines' three major unions engineered a deal whereby they obtained a majority of the troubled airline's
shares. A few years later, unions and management were still at logger-
heads, and the company was plunged into bankruptcy.

What was going on here? Evidently, there was more to successful
employee ownership than stock ownership itself. Unless that was better understood, there might be little reason for anybody to support
measures to expand it.

4

The Quest for Cooperation

In assessing United Airlines' brief and calamitous experiment with employee ownership—the experiment ended with the airline's filing for bankruptcy protection in December 2002—it helps to go back to 1995.

That was a good year for United. It was the first year of the new ESOP, which owned 55 percent of the company. It was also the best year for public shareholders in United's seventy-year history. The stock outperformed the Standard & Poor's 500 index by 67 percent. Shareholder value increased by more than $4 billion. Some of the outstanding performance seemed traceable to a new attitude among employees. Grievances had fallen 74 percent, sick time 17 percent. Revenue per employee—a key measure of productivity in the industry—had risen 10 percent. Surveys showed that employees liked working at United. "People were happy to come to work," remembered a veteran mechanic. Television commercials run during the Super Bowl featured smartly dressed United pilots and mechanics under the heading "We Don't Just Work Here."

The changes could be seen not just in attitudes and advertising but in behavior on the job. Task teams involving employees from all over the company began attacking workplace problems and figuring out how to cut costs. A team studying fuel consumption, for example, recommended half a dozen ways that the airline could save money. Meanwhile, "everyone from gate agents to mechanics gained new authority to address customer complaints without consulting their supervisors," as the *Chicago Tribune* reported in a comprehensive retrospective published in 2003.[1] Mechanics were allowed to sign off on repair work that once would have required an inspector's OK. Anyone who saw a better way of doing something was encouraged to suggest changes. Even pilots got into the act, performing tasks like clearing food trays to shorten turnaround time on the ground.[2]

Five years later, the teams were long gone; in fact, the company had disbanded them just a year after establishing them. Gone, too, was the cooperative attitude. That year—the summer of 2000—pilots seeking a new wage deal staged a ferocious slowdown. They refused to fly overtime, making it impossible for the airline to keep to its schedule. They taxied at a crawl. They flew low in order to burn *more* fuel. One pilot "walked off a full 747, claiming nerves." Another announced that he wanted to recheck his instruments, and kept the plane on the tarmac for three hours. On-time performance, which had reached 81 percent the year the ESOP was put in place, dropped to an industry-worst 61 percent for the year. (It was at 40 percent during the summer.) The airline experienced "a fourfold increase in delays caused by pilots insisting on repairing inconsequential items, like a broken coffee maker or a burned out reading light." Passenger traffic plunged. The pilots as a group still owned some 25 percent of the airline, but never mind: as one reporter wrote, "they were sabotaging their own company."[3]

The turnabout in employee attitudes was hardly the only reason for United's bankruptcy filing in 2002. The company had prospered during the 1990s partly because of the dot-com boom in and around Silicon Valley. At one point, trips to and from California accounted for some 40 percent of its revenue.[4] So United was hit especially hard when the dot-coms collapsed and the rest of the tech industry sagged. Then came September 11, 2001, when United lost two of its planes and their crews to terrorists and subsequently found itself in the worst period ever for air travel. Still, employee attitudes played a part in the bankruptcy, and not just through the infamous slowdown of 2000. Disillusioned with the way the ESOP was working out (or not working out) in the 1990s, United's powerful unions had pushed to restore their previous wage levels, raising the airline's costs to among the industry's highest. When the crunch came after 9/11, the company had no cushion to fall back on.

A GOOD IDEA GONE WRONG

How the ESOP's high hopes and promise were brought so low is a tale worth a book of its own. But any account would have to focus on at least three phases.

Divisive Beginnings

It's a widely held belief that the idea for employee ownership at United came from its management team. In fact, it came from the employees, the pilots in particular. The pilots' union at United—the Air Line Pilots Association, or ALPA—had been interested in buying control of the company ever since 1985. That year, union members were forced back to work after a particularly bitter strike, and lawyer F. Lee Bailey urged the pilots to consider demanding stock whenever they had to make concessions. Eventually, Bailey argued, the pilots could get majority control. An aggressive young ALPA leader named Rick Dubinsky took Bailey's advice to heart and tried on three separate occasions to engineer a pilot-led employee buyout of the airline. When the ESOP deal was finally done, in 1994, it entailed huge concessions. ALPA and the International Association of Machinists—which had joined the buyout effort out of fear that then-CEO Stephen M. Wolf wanted to abolish many union members' jobs—gave back some $4.8 billion in prospective wages and benefits. In return, the two unions and the company's nonunionized employees got 55 percent of the airline's stock, plus the right to name three members of the board of directors. But was the stock worth the givebacks? Plenty of union members complained that it wasn't. Meanwhile, the flight attendants' union never joined the buyout at all, on the grounds that its members couldn't afford wage concessions. The phrase "You can't eat stock" would become a watchword of those who opposed the whole deal.

Fading Support

Still, the ESOP began amid high hopes. New CEO Gerald Greenwald, picked with union approval as a condition of the deal, set about cultivating labor support. Managers within the company launched those task teams. Rank-and-file employees allowed themselves to think things might be different, and began to act accordingly. But changing any large, entrenched organization is hard; it requires constant pressure. No pressure was forthcoming. ALPA, still riven with controversy over the givebacks, voted out Dubinsky ally Roger Hall, who had taken over as union head when Dubinsky's term expired. The union's new leadership had its own priorities, notably a new approach to collective bargaining called "interest-based bargaining," and little interest in employee ownership. The machinists, never too excited about employee ownership to begin with, became increasingly distracted by a challenge from a rival union and so contributed little. At the company itself, says Chris Mackin, an employee-ownership consultant who worked with United at the time, "a cluster of 'old guard' management officials who openly criticized the original move to employee ownership began to gain strength." The new "vice president of people"—he once would have been known as vice president for human resources—was hired with support from the new ALPA regime and was more interested in that new bargaining strategy than in the ESOP. In fact, he declared himself "not enthusiastic" about the whole idea of ownership. "I sat across from the newly installed vice president of the people division of the largest employee-owned company in history who, incredibly, was making no secret of his antipathy toward employee ownership," remembers Mackin. "Not a good omen."[5]

Downward Spiral

The structure of the deal worked against it from the beginning. Not only were the flight attendants on the outside looking in, but those who were part of the ESOP would get stock for only five years. New employees who joined the company after that time would get none at all. By 1999, the ESOP wasn't anyone's priority. "Labor didn't hold management's feet to the fire," says Dubinsky, who was reelected chairman of ALPA in 1999 but had been out of office during the critical years. "So management ran a traditional company—as traditional as any company in America. I sat on the board for two years, and in two years' time there wasn't 20 minutes' discussion of employee ownership." In 1999 and 2000, with the ESOP flagging and contract negotiations coming up, Dubinsky was in no mood for compromise. He "reminded his pilots that they weren't obligated to fly overtime, as they normally did, and that they should fly 'to the letter of our agreement'—a euphemism for going slow."[6] Then James Goodwin, the CEO who had replaced

Greenwald, announced that he had negotiated a merger with US Airways, a move that would jeopardize United pilots' seniority. Infuriated, the pilots mounted their slowdown. Before long the company caved, giving them an immediate raise ranging from 22 to 28 percent, plus successive 4.5 percent raises every year thereafter until 2004. (The proposed merger was subsequently nixed by the Justice Department on antitrust grounds.)

September 11, of course, was a blow that left the entire airline industry reeling. But United was hit harder than some of its competitors, for the reasons mentioned earlier. In October 2001, Goodwin issued a memo saying that the airline could "perish." That seemed like just one more strong-arm tactic to the embittered employees, and labor's allies on the board forced Goodwin out. The CEOs who followed were finally able to win new wage concessions from the unions. But for the airline it was too little, too late. When the U.S. government rejected United's request for loan guarantees, in late 2002, bankruptcy court was the only option.

So what is the lesson of United's experience? As we noted earlier, it is as foolish to argue that employee ownership caused the debacle as it is to claim that investor ownership caused, say, US Airways' equally grim trajectory into bankruptcy. Anyone who wants to argue that ESOPs lead to failure must account for the thousands of ESOP companies that are thriving. But employee ownership certainly didn't save United, either, as so many people had hoped it would. Why not? What was missing? Granted, there was bad blood all around. But why did it persist? And even if both sides had wanted the ESOP to succeed, would the task teams and the other innovations initiated in 1995 have done the trick? What else might the company and the unions have done to get people thinking and acting like owners?

As it happens, these are questions with a history all their own, dating back nearly a century. A traditional business contemplates distinct roles for two separate groups of people. In one group are those who provide the equity financing for the enterprise and who therefore receive ownership rights. In the other are those hired to do the work. Enterprises typically exist for the purpose of benefiting only the owners. This is not only a matter of culture and practice, it's a matter of law. Those in charge of a corporation have a fiduciary duty to serve the best interests of the owners and may be sued if they stray from that obligation. But the structure presents an obvious dilemma: the employees are left with little inherent interest in the enterprise's performance and thus have little motivation to work diligently, creatively, energetically, or proactively. Management's traditional solution to the dilemma was to give workers detailed instructions and then supervise them closely to make sure they were doing what they were told. Workers often chafed under such conditions and expressed their displeasure in all manner of means, ranging from sneaking naps to organizing unions to outright theft and sabotage.

The proponents of co-ops and stock ownership, including Kelso, believed that they had *the* answer to this "labor question": just make the workers into owners. But the experience of companies that tried out various forms of employee ownership, down to and including United Airlines, didn't always bear out that belief. In some cases employee ownership seemed to make little difference, as the labor economist Sumner Slichter had predicted way back in 1929. In other cases it blew up in its proponents' faces, as at United. Meanwhile, several other schools of management thought and experimentation were taking a different approach to the labor question. The issue, they argued, wasn't so much *ownership*, though that might help; it was how a company was *run*. At various points during the past century, people came up with a variety of ideas about how to run a business more cooperatively, in hopes of bringing about labor peace and creating a more productive enterprise. The legacies of their different quests are visible in U.S. business today, and the equity model borrows elements from nearly all.

INDUSTRIAL DEMOCRACY

"The employees must have the opportunity of participating in the decisions as to what shall be their condition and how the business shall be run," declared Louis Brandeis before the Senate Commission on Industrial Relations in 1915. Brandeis, who would be named to the Supreme Court by Woodrow Wilson a year later, was already a familiar and well-respected public figure in the United States. He was also a partisan of what was known at the time as *industrial democracy*. Questioned by a commissioner as to whether he really meant that employees should have a voice in management, Brandeis replied that he did indeed: "not only a voice but a vote; not merely a right to be heard, but a position through which labor may participate in management."[7]

To page through the historical documents of Brandeis's era is to come across a surprising number of companies that actually tried to implement industrial democracy in some form. Most of these companies created "works councils" or "industrial councils" that included a handful of employee representatives. A number of the councils had no more than an advisory role. But other companies obviously had grander visions, modeling their industrial democracies after the structure of the U.S. government itself. Two remarkable examples are the Riverside and Dan River Cotton Mills, in Danville, Virginia, and Goodyear Tire & Rubber, in Akron, Ohio.[8]

Both companies' plans were set up in 1919. At Riverside and Dan River, the organization consisted of a house, elected by and from the employees through secret ballot; a senate, appointed by the company's officers; and a cabinet, comprising the officers themselves. Either legislative body could originate a "bill," but to take effect, the bill had to be approved by all three bodies. (Sample bill, introduced and passed in 1920: "That a rule be made and enforced to require each and every person to look at his imperfect work insofar as practicable . . . [and] that when such a rule is enforced the weaver will not be asked to answer for so many things that he has no control over.") Like the U.S. Congress, the organization had plenty of committees, including bonus and dividends, ways and means, adjustments and complaints, and constitutional questions.[9] Goodyear's plan—created by an employee commission, sanctioned by management, and approved by an 82 percent majority in an employee referendum—was equally ambitious. It divided the company along departmental lines into forty precincts. It gave voting rights to every U.S. citizen over eighteen who had been with the company at least six months. The industrial assembly, as it was called, included both a house and a senate. If the two bodies passed a bill, the matter went to the factory manager for his signature. If the manager failed to sign the legislation, the assembly could appeal to the company's board of directors. (One such bill in 1922 secured an across-the-board wage increase for employees.) The assembly met regularly with the company's managers to discuss Goodyear's financial situation and major strategic issues.[10]

These experiments shouldn't be viewed out of context. It was a time of intense labor strife in the United States. The Bolshevik revolution had established a communist regime in Russia. More than a few corporate leaders hoped that some form of industrial democracy would defuse the more radical and potentially more threatening trend toward unionization. For that reason alone, the plans drew considerable opposition from labor and its supporters. But neither should the plans be written off as purely cynical moves on management's part. Organizations such as Goodyear's were popular among their constituents and were effective vehicles for protecting employee interests. The Goodyear assembly, for example, was put to a referendum of workers five years after its creation and was again approved by more than four-fifths of the voters. "Most Goodyear employees seem to have viewed the Industrial Assembly as a useful, reasonably assertive organization," acknowledges the labor historian Daniel Nelson.[11] There was, moreover, more than a touch of idealism in the air about reforming labor relations, and it was affecting companies of all sorts and sizes, whether or not they were union targets. Thus the owners of a six-hundred-employee company called Dutchess Bleachery, in Wappingers Falls, New York, adopted a "partnership plan" in 1918 that provided several avenues for employee participation in management, just as Brandeis had advocated:

> Not only does the Partnership Plan afford representation to employes [sic] in determining the conditions of their employment, but it admits to the Board of Directors a representative of the wage-earners in the mill, turns over entirely to a Board of Operatives the administration of the company's houses, assigns definite responsibility for shop management to a Board of Managers composed of six officers of the company and of six wage-earners, provides employes with information concerning the financial condition and conduct of the business, and includes a representative of the townspeople of Wappingers Falls in the Board of Directors.[12]

The Bleachery functioned successfully under this system for many years.

WELFARE CAPITALISM

Industrial democracy as practiced by Goodyear and the others mostly died out with the Depression. Like the ownership schemes described in the previous chapter, the hopes and dreams of cooperation couldn't survive the wholesale wage cuts and layoffs of the 1930s. Then, too, as the union movement gained power, it lobbied to have all such organizations outlawed as "company unions." The Wagner Act—passed in 1935 and upheld by the Supreme Court in 1937—did just that. Henceforth it would be illegal in the United States for companies to establish any employee organization empowered to deal with wages, hours, and working conditions, a restriction that has plagued participatory-management efforts ever since. Still, occasional vestiges of the industrial democracy model may be found today, as in a handful of ESOP companies that permit employees to elect board members.

But though that historical rivulet largely dried up, a broader and often intermingling stream dwindled but revived. Industrial democracy was one part of a broader movement known as *welfare capitalism*.

Welfare capitalism's main idea, writes historian Sanford M. Jacoby, was that "corporations would shield workers from the strains of industrialism."[13] Originally known as "welfare work" and limited to such measures as setting up company towns, the movement grew to encompass employee educational and recreational programs, financial benefits such as insurance plans and pensions, and profit sharing, as well as experiments in industrial democracy and stock ownership. It wasn't just altruism, of course: corporate leaders hoped that such measures would create a more stable, more dedicated, and hence more productive workforce. According to the conventional view, all such measures also died out in the 1930s—but that, says Jacoby, is an oversimplification. Thus "vanguard" companies such as AT&T, DuPont, IBM, Procter & Gamble, and Standard Oil of New Jersey maintained a number of their welfare measures well into the postwar era.

The prime example of such a company—Jacoby calls it a "paragon of welfare capitalism"—was Eastman Kodak Company, headquartered in Rochester, New York. Curiously, Kodak never did much with employee representation. It had set up a controversial plan at its Camera

Works in 1919 allowing workers to meet with management over griev-
ances, but George Eastman soon declared himself totally opposed to
any form of industrial representation. The plan was discontinued in
the mid-1920s.[14] What Kodak did do was lavish benefits on its employees, provide them with the opportunity to make good money, and
manage them astutely. As early as 1897, Eastman introduced an employee suggestion system and awarded monthly prizes for the best suggestion. Not long after, the company began providing

> . . . a slew of traditional welfare activities for men and women
> —dining halls, smoking rooms, reading rooms, recreation pro-
> grams, and an assembly hall for concerts and dances . . . In
> 1910 Kodak established the Athletic Association, which elected
> its own officers and charged a membership fee of only one dol-
> lar. In return, members could use the company's tennis courts,
> baseball diamonds, cinder track, and basketball gymnasium.
> Activities were hierarchically inclusive: production workers
> sang and played alongside foremen and managers.[15]

George Eastman supplemented such benefits with generous financial rewards, giving his own stock to employees and endowing an employees' association. The association provided disability and accident
insurance, benefits to sick and injured workers, and retirement bonuses.
In 1912 he created a profit-sharing plan, known as the wage dividend
plan, which was tied to the dividend payments to shareholders. A worker
with five years of service typically enjoyed an extra month's worth of
pay every year from this source.[16]

Kodak expanded nearly all these benefits during the 1920s and, unlike most companies, was able to maintain most of them during the
1930s. After the war, the company determined to maintain its reputation as a leader and introduced some new benefit nearly every year. It
built an eighteen-hole golf course and a huge recreation center, including "three cafeterias, meeting rooms, bowling alleys, squash courts,
pool tables, a gymnasium, retiree lounge, pistol range, and auditorium
that showed movies daily." Dozens of company sports teams, bowling
leagues, and golf leagues "sent a powerful message of corporate unity."[17]
Meanwhile—aware that poor supervision in the plant could under-
mine that message of unity—it spent considerable sums on training

foremen in human relations, and it monitored their behavior through locked suggestion boxes placed in every plant. If a foreman was found to be treating employees poorly, the company took quick and decisive action. But it also made sure that foremen themselves were well treated, sponsoring a foremen's club with dinners, smokers, and musical entertainment.[18] Throughout, Kodak did its best to reduce status distinctions. It "refused to pay special benefits to managers, ran all benefit programs (including time off) on a company-wide basis, and taught supervisors to say 'so-and-so works "with me," not "for me."'"[19]

All such policies call to mind the companies today that make lists such as the "100 Best Companies to Work For," published annually by *Fortune* magazine. "Best Companies" organizations such as SAS Institute, a North Carolina software company that offers employees a truly amazing array of benefits, are today's Kodaks. Kodak itself maintains a generous benefits package even now, including the wage dividend. What it has not been able to do, however, is guarantee job security. Forced by economic conditions to abandon its long-standing no-layoff policy, Kodak shrank its Rochester-area workforce from sixty thousand four hundred people in 1982 (representing 19 percent of the county's jobs) to twenty-one thousand (6 percent) twenty years later.[20]

HUMAN RELATIONS AND THE HIGH-PERFORMANCE WORKPLACE

Industrial democracy and welfare capitalism operated primarily at the level of the whole enterprise. They attempted to create a spirit of cooperation throughout the company. The human relations school of management, which derived from the famous experiments of Fritz Roethlisberger and Elton Mayo at Western Electric's Hawthorne Works in Cicero, Illinois, focused on the work group itself. Every beginning management student learns of the "Hawthorne effect." The experimenters turned up the illumination as a group of test workers did their jobs, and found that productivity went up. They turned down the lights—and productivity went up then, too. "The workers seemed to be responding more to the attention they were receiving from management than to any physical change in their environment," as one account puts it. "This response of the workers was called 'the Hawthorne effect.'"[21] Central to the effect was the fact that someone was listening to people who weren't usually listened to. Workers themselves got a chance to express their opinions about working conditions, and about changes in the pace and organization of work. In fact, they "got so used to determining their own conditions of work that when their suggestions were occasionally overruled, they complained vociferously to management and to the investigators." At one point the operators—all women—said they wanted the experiment to go on indefinitely, because they preferred working in the test room to working in the regular department. The experiment's observer, who was as close as the test-room employees had to a supervisor, suggested that conditions in both places were much the same. The workers disagreed:

> *Op. 3:* "Yes, there are too many bosses in the [regular] department."

> *Op. 1:* "Yes, Mr. —— [the observer] is the only boss we have."

> *Op. 2:* "Say, he's no boss. We don't have any boss."

> *Observer (starting to speak):* "But, you know . . ."

> *Op. 3:* "Shut up" [said good-naturedly].

> *Op. 2:* "Look at that. Look at the way she tells her boss to shut up."

Mayo observed, "Many times over, the history sheets and other records [in the test room] show that in the opinion of the group all supervision had been removed."[22]

The hallmark of the human relations school, later developed further by numerous theorists including Abraham Maslow and Douglas McGregor, was just that: insofar as possible, *employees should manage themselves* rather than simply do what a supervisor tells them to do. They should take responsibility for their own work. They should decide—or at least have a voice in—matters such as scheduling, working conditions, and how the work is organized. The notion (with various theoretical accoutrements differing from one thinker to another) has been dubbed "eupsychian management" (Maslow), Theory Y (McGregor), socio-technical systems (Eric Trist and others associated with the Tavistock Institute in the United Kingdom), quality of worklife (a euphemism popular in the 1970s), and, most commonly, participative or participatory management.[23] Peter Drucker, perhaps the most influential writer in the history of American management, was reflecting and advocating the human relations approach when he wrote in his pioneering 1954 book *The Practice of Management*, "The worker should be enabled to control, measure and guide his own performance. He should know how he is doing without being told . . . The worker will assume responsibility for peak performance only if he has a managerial vision, that is, if he sees the enterprise as if he were a manager responsible, through his performance, for its success and survival. This vision he can only attain through the experience of participation."[24]

Companies adopting the theory, in whatever form, often found themselves transforming the entire workplace to accommodate it. Thus the General Foods pet-food plant in Topeka, Kansas—a legendary workplace in the annals of participative management—was designed around a system of semiautonomous work teams, "facilitative" leadership, and information sharing. (The approach came to be known as the Topeka System.) "Autonomy means [employees] have to be able to plan the work, check the quality, change the design of the jobs," declared the plant manager. "They have to have real control, not just over simple stuff, like when to take a coffee break—it's the real guts of the job."[25] And an aerospace company called Non-Linear Systems (NLS), which early-PC aficionados will remember in its later incarnation as developer of the Kaypro personal computer, restructured its factory after owner Andrew Kay read Maslow's book *Motivation and Personality*. When Maslow visited NLS, in 1962,

> The assembly line had been dismantled, and the workers had been organized in teams of six to seven, with each team being responsible for the entire process of manufacturing, including assembly, inspection, and debugging. The teams set their own work hours, as well as the production schedule. There were no time cards.[26]

Today, of course, the human relations or participative management school lives on in the various practices that go under the rubric of high-performance work systems. The phrase is vague, but it generally refers to one or more of the following: work teams or cells with at least partial responsibility for managing themselves; bottom-up quality practices, such as the expectation that a worker will interrupt production if he or she notices a defect; and active participation by employees in coming up with, and implementing, ideas for improvement. The goals include greater worker satisfaction (and thus lower turnover), better quality, and higher productivity. High-performance work systems of one kind or another have been instituted in dozens of different industries, albeit more in manufacturing than in service, and in many hundreds of individual facilities. The best-known example is probably New United Motor Manufacturing, Inc. (NUMMI), the Toyota–General Motors joint venture in Fremont, California, which has outperformed even the most technologically advanced of GM's other plants. But NUMMI, which allowed for only limited worker participation, was relatively modest in its aims, compared with similar experiments in industries such as steel. In a "large unionized sheet mill in the northeastern United States"—the researchers who visited it agreed not to name the company—"natural work groups" elect their own team captains and come up with their own ideas for meeting short-term performance goals.[27]

These human relations experiments and their descendants have had a checkered history. The Topeka pet-food plant became a kind of political football within General Foods: eventually its managers were transferred elsewhere, and a new manager was given the marching orders "Cut this missionary crap."[28] Later the plant was sold and resold—though its eventual owner, Heinz, suddenly and unexpectedly announced that the Topeka System would be maintained. Andrew Kay, of Non-Linear Systems, maintained his Maslovian approach until the mid-1970s; then, faced with a sharp business downturn, he "reintroduced traditional management practices."[29] This is a common reaction to hard times, and one we don't totally understand; presumably the new practices were working, or else he wouldn't have maintained them that long. So why eliminate them just because business is bad? Our best guess is that the fear associated with a business downturn led to contentiousness, as at Columbia Conserve, and the contentiousness undermined the new practices.

High-performance work systems are common in U.S. plants today but are by no means universal. "Changing to high-involvement work is hard," declared two professors who studied the systems extensively. "Successful change is rare, and variance in work practice is widespread."[30]

Still, the idea hasn't lost its appeal. In late 2003, wrote *BusinessWeek*, the International Association of Machinists union at Boeing was "pushing an initiative called High Performance Work Organization, which gives workers more responsibility for making continuous productivity improvements. Execs at Harley-Davidson, Inc. and International Specialty Products, a maker of chemicals and pharmaceuticals, credit the initiative for helping to revitalize inefficient factories." Boeing CEO Harry Stonecipher was said to be "amenable" to the idea.[31]

THE SCANLON PLAN

Of course, many such experiments overlapped with one another. Thus Western Electric, site of the Hawthorne experiments, was also a leading exemplar of welfare capitalism. Shop-floor participation schemes were often (not always) supplemented or complemented with various sorts of incentive or variable compensation, such as profit sharing, bonuses, and stock. Non-Linear Systems, for example, not only rearranged the organization of its workplace, it also "paid 25 percent more than the prevailing wage and was among the first companies to offer its employees stock options."[32]

This may be the place to drop in a word about one of the more unusual efforts to bring about labor-management cooperation, one that originated in another era but survives to this day. The Scanlon approach was notable because it explicitly tied performance improvements from employee participation to more money for the employees who were doing the improving.

Joe Scanlon, like Louis Kelso, has become something of a legend among a very small group of people. (There isn't really a term for a person whose name is a household word in only a handful of households.) Also like Kelso, he led a life that was a collection of seeming contradictions. Though short in stature, he became a prizefighter. Though once a prizefighter, he became a cost accountant. Though once an accountant, he went to work in a steel mill, Empire Steel, and rose to become president of the local union. In 1937 the mill was in trouble, and Scanlon's local asked for advice from Clinton S. Golden, a labor leader who was a partisan of industrial democracy. Figure out how to tap the knowledge of the workers themselves, advised Golden. No one knows how to do the job as well as they do. Scanlon devised a plan for gathering ideas from the workers, many of which were then implemented. Soon Empire was back in the black, and its workers got a raise. Golden "was so impressed by Scanlon that in 1938 he brought the Irishman to Pittsburgh and put him in charge of helping other troubled companies and their union locals develop participation programs."[33] Douglas McGregor traveled to Pittsburgh to observe Scanlon's work. Equally impressed, he invited Scanlon to join the faculty of the Massachusetts Institute of Technology, where he remained until his untimely death in 1956.

At MIT, Scanlon continued to work with companies, putting into place what came to be known as Scanlon Plans. In fact, the name was a misnomer: there was no such thing as the Scanlon Plan, Joe used to tell people, only a set of principles that could be applied in a variety of ways.[34] Even the principles themselves seem rather fluid, depending on who is summarizing them and when they are doing so. But a bare-bones synopsis would include at least three points. Employees and management together establish a baseline marker, such as current labor costs or output per worker. Both groups, but particularly the employees, join committees or hold meetings to suggest improvements in the work process, with an eye toward improving performance against the baseline. If performance improves, the financial gain goes into a pool, to be divided among the company itself, management, and employees. (The Scanlon approach is thus an example of what is known as gainsharing.) Scanlon Plans in the steel industry died out during World War II, apparent victims of managerial intransigence and fear of losing control. But many other large companies, including Dana Corporation and General Motors, adopted them in the postwar era.[35] Even today, several dozen companies regard themselves as Scanlon companies: they belong to an association, hold an annual conference to exchange ideas, and practice Joe Scanlon's original principles in about as many different ways as Christians worship their deity.

CULTURE

As you may have noticed, all the approaches discussed so far in this chapter involve organizational changes—different benefits, different decision-making structures, and so on. They all are vulnerable to what might be called the Bill Fowler problem.

Fowler was a factory worker who was written up by the *Wall Street Journal*'s Timothy Aeppel a few years ago. His employer was a company called Blackmer/Dover Resources, Inc., in Grand Rapids, Michigan. His job was to cut metal shafts for industrial pumps. Cutting the shafts was a precision task: "a minor error could render a pump useless." Fowler's cuts were known for their exceptional accuracy, and he could do machine changeovers hours faster than anybody else. So did management ask him to share his secrets with others? Yes, indeed: "We've realized . . . we need to start asking these guys what they know," said the president. And did Fowler comply? Not a chance. "If I gave away my tricks, management could use [them] to speed things up and keep me at a flat-out pace all day long," declared Fowler. Said a coworker, "He hardly ever has made a suggestion for an improvement."[36]

Frederick W. Taylor's system of scientific management attempted to discover the secrets of exceptional workers such as Fowler and to incorporate them into a plant's standard work practices. But it wasn't very successful, for much the same reason that Fowler's employer hadn't been successful: workers feared giving away their tricks. Purely structural change—a new team-based system, for instance—is unlikely to persuade the Bill Fowlers of the world to work with a more enthusiastic and cooperative attitude. Fowler and people like him have to *want* to share their tricks. They have to *identify* with the company, *feel* like part of the group, *care* about the business's success. Soft stuff, no doubt—but it is just such "soft" characteristics that define some of the business world's most successful corporate cultures.

The notion of corporate culture goes back to the writings of Chester A. Barnard, a management theorist whose day job was to serve as president of New Jersey Bell, one of the operating companies that were then part of AT&T. Barnard, who wrote in the 1930s, didn't use the term *culture*, but he wrote about a company's "informal organization"—its "customs, mores, folklore, social norms and ideals."[37] In the 1980s two McKinsey & Company consultants named Thomas J. Peters (later reincarnated as plain old Tom Peters) and Robert H. Waterman resurrected the notion in their book *In Search of Excellence*, which became one of the best-selling management manuals of all time. In their eyes, culture wasn't just a part of a company, it was a key requirement for business success. "Without exception, the dominance and coherence of culture proved to be an essential quality of the excellent companies," they wrote.[38] At about the same time, Terrence E. Deal and Allan A. Kennedy—Kennedy was ex-McKinsey—came out with a whole book devoted to the idea, one that implicitly addressed the Bill Fowler problem. Employees at companies with strong cultures, they observed, express "an unusual degree of loyalty and commitment to the company." One employee they interviewed said, "My goals follow the company's. It's the company and I. I think that's pretty true of everyone."[39]

Peters and Waterman wrote about big companies that preached and lived well-defined sets of values: Walt Disney Company, 3M Worldwide, IBM, and others. Deal and Kennedy added in up-and-comers such as Tandem Computer Company, a manufacturer of computer systems. Neither pair wrote about the company that was arguably creating one of the strongest cultures anywhere and that turned out to be the most up-and-coming of any up-and-comers: Wal-Mart Stores.

Like its founder, Sam Walton—"Mr. Sam" to the company's associates—Wal-Mart was *sui generis*, a company unlike any other. It grew up in America's small towns, staying under the radar of big competitors such as Kmart. It focused relentlessly on buying and selling its wares as cheaply as possible, day in and day out ("everyday low prices"). Over time it developed an unparalleled information system that let its managers know exactly what was selling, where, and when, and it has famously used that information, along with its ever-growing scale, to dictate terms to its suppliers. Walton himself was hardly your run-of-the-mill successful entrepreneur. Though rich beyond imagination, he continued to live in Bentonville, Arkansas, and drove around town in a pickup, his hunting dogs on the front seat. Both Walton and the company he founded were known not just for retailing savvy but for creating a folksy, friendly culture in the workplace. In his autobiography, Walton wrote, "If you're good to people, and fair with them, and demanding of them, they will eventually decide that they're on your side."[40] Walton regularly visited stores to chat with employees. He led them in the famous Wal-Mart cheer ("Give me a W!" etc.). He promised an open-door policy, time and a half for Sunday work, good chances for promotion, and the opportunity to buy Wal-Mart stock. Many employees responded by going an extra mile—in however loopy a fashion—to help the company realize its goals. Walton wrote proudly in his autobiography of many such examples, including this one:

> Our New Iberia, Louisiana, store fields a cheerleading squad called the Shrinkettes. Their cheers deal mostly with, what else? cutting shrinkage: *"WHAT DO YOU DO ABOUT SHRINK-AGE? CRUSH IT! CRUSH IT!"* The Shrinkettes stole the show at one of our annual meetings with cheers like: *"CALIFORNIA ORANGES, TEXAS CACTUS, WE THINK KMART COULD USE SOME PRACTICE!"*[41]

"Walton's deal," wrote *Fortune*'s Mark Gimein, "promised that cost-cutting could coexist with a moral center—that Wal-Mart could be both the cheapest place to shop and the best place to work."[42] Wal-Mart's culture, said another observer, was "the glue that kept employees enthusiastically loyal and kept the stores striving to meet the high standards set by Sam Walton."[43]

The fate of strong-culture companies may be an object lesson in the vulnerabilities of this approach to the labor question. Disney, 3M, and IBM have all had their troubles in recent years. Tandem was acquired by Compaq Computer Corporation. Plenty of other Silicon Valley enterprises with a work-hard, play-hard, do-it-for-the-company culture are also long gone. For its part, Wal-Mart is a phenomenally successful business, and its culture is hardly dead. For example, it was still making *Fortune*'s "100 Best Companies to Work For" list as late as 2002. Still, there is good evidence that the company's culture has weakened substantially over the years and that many employees are unhappy: "They no longer believe Wal-Mart and its managers are on their side," Gimein reports. Signs of the discontent include big matters, such as sex-discrimination suits and union-organizing drives. They also include the small but not trivial on-the-job grievance:

> Every manager is at war with us [an employee in Iowa complained]. To do my job, I need a little piece of equipment that costs $7 or $8. It's called a swift tagger. It's what I use to put the

labels on all the clothing. I've been there a year, and I can't have one. The managers hide them. They don't have enough of them. The managers hide it for fear of someone else hiding it from them.

And:

A year and a half ago, [the store management] said they would have to start doing more with less. [This is from a manager in Pennsylvania.] They would start trimming back the amount of help you had. Where I had maybe six or seven people, I would be cut down to four. The assistant managers were told, "You guys will have to work a six-day week, mandatory." They really didn't care how much of a toll it took on the employees.[44]

Wal-Mart's culture thrived when "Mr. Sam" was alive and when the company was primarily a small-town, rural-America phenomenon. Now that it is international in scope, with many urban stores, it operates more like a conventional business, and it has chosen to focus on keeping its labor costs low. A particular irony for this book is the fact that Wal-Mart traditionally made stock available at a 15 percent discount to its employees, and many who worked for the company in the early years grew rich by buying up what was then a cheap stock. Today the company continues the program, but most workers can't afford to buy any stock. According to a report on PBS, "Not one in 50 workers has amassed as much as $50,000 through the stock-ownership pension plan."[45]

OPEN-BOOK MANAGEMENT

This chapter wouldn't be complete without a brief synopsis of the most recent and in many ways the most innovative approach to the labor question. Open-book management is a critical element of the equity model, and we'll discuss it in greater detail in chapter 7. But it's worth remembering where it came from—not a professor or a consultant, but a company leader in desperate straits, who was forced to come up with a new way of running a business.

In the early 1980s, a Chicago native named Jack Stack was managing what was known as the Springfield Renew Center, in Springfield, Missouri. The plant—a small unit of the big company then known as International Harvester, now Navistar International—remanufactured heavy-duty diesel engines. But times had been hard. Battered by foreign competition and desperate for cash, Harvester was in negotiations to sell off the plant to another big manufacturer. Stack and a handful of other managers had also put in an offer, which Harvester had ignored for more than a year. But when the negotiations with the other buyer suddenly broke down, Harvester turned around and accepted the managers' offer— and gave them six weeks to put together a buyout package. Together the group came up with $100,000 in equity investment. Unfortunately, they needed $7 million to close the deal and another $2 million in working capital if the new company was to have a prayer of surviving. On the off chance that his bid might be accepted, Stack had been contacting banks for a loan; he found that the answer was no, no, and no again, until a lender for Bank of America finally signed on for a $6 million loan and a $2 million credit line. When Harvester agreed to accept an IOU for $1 million, a new company was born. Formally known as Springfield Re-Manufacturing Center Corporation, it was always just called "SRC." (Its full name today is SRC Holdings Corporation.) SRC was owned by its managers and employees, for one of the first moves Stack made was to set up an ESOP. But it was also, as Stack likes to say, "near-comatose." It quickly ran through its credit line, giving it a debt-to-equity ratio of 89 to 1. If it didn't make the bank payment each month, it would go under.

So Stack tried something unusual. He began making sure all of his managers understood the financials. The key line on the balance sheet, of course, was "cash," because that was what determined whether the fledgling company could make the bank payment. He also asked his managers to begin helping the people they supervised understand the numbers, and so on down the line. After a year in business, Stack created what he called a game: as a group, managers and employees would shoot for reducing the debt from $7.2 million, as it was then, to $4.2 million. To make sure they didn't sacrifice profitability just to reduce the debt, they would also aim for $2.2 million in pretax profit. If they hit both goals, the company would pay out $300,000 in bonuses, or about 8 percent of total pay.

For the next twelve months, they played that game:

The entire team worked overtime to make sure people understood the game and the goals and knew what they had to do to
win. In the process, we all became teachers, especially those of
us with a somewhat better grasp of the numbers.

For example, I put our standard cost accountant, Doug
Rothert, in charge of production, which came as a shock to
him since he had no experience in manufacturing. I told him
not to worry: His job was to teach finance to the people in the
plant. He began conducting almost daily tutorials with individual supervisors, going through work orders, showing how
the numbers flowed back to the income statement and how the
income statement flowed into the balance sheet. The supervisors then went out and did the same thing with the hourly
people.

Meanwhile, the other managers ran training sessions of their
own, and we talked up the game at every chance we got. Our
CFO, Dan McCoy, would regularly go on the public address system to give updates on the score. At the end of each quarter, we'd
hold a series of informational meetings throughout the company to review the results with all of the employees.[46]

SRC came close to winning its game that year and paid its employees most of the bonus they had earned. But it was the long-term effect
that was more dramatic. The company kept up the information sharing, along with the informal instruction on how a business works. It
began to hold weekly meetings ("huddles") to compile the data that
would go into the financials. Those meetings began to project what
the financials would look like over the coming weeks and months. The
company also developed a sophisticated bonus system that tied payouts
to improvements in key financial figures, and made sure that managers
were out on the floor explaining exactly what was involved. Shop-floor
employees began to understand how their performance on the job contributed (or didn't contribute) to the success of the business.

The phrase *open-book management* actually originated in a 1990
Inc. magazine article by John Case about three other companies that
shared financial information with employees.[47] Those companies and,

since then, many hundreds of others have developed homegrown open-book systems. Only some of them resemble SRC's approach. The wide variety of experience is detailed in John Case's books *Open-Book Management: The Coming Business Revolution* (1995) and *The Open-Book Experience* (1998).[48] Still, SRC was the pioneer, and Stack the key innovator. When the company began offering seminars about its system to other businesspeople, thousands signed up. SRC, said *BusinessWeek*, had become a "mecca" for new management thinking. It remains so today.

COMBINING OWNERSHIP AND EMPLOYEE INVOLVEMENT

Common sense suggests that it might be a good idea to combine ownership, whether through an ESOP or some other device, with one or another of the mechanisms designed to encourage employees to work cooperatively and enthusiastically. Many of the innovators did precisely that. Thus Andrew Kay offered stock options while he was rearranging the production line. Jack Stack combined an ESOP with his open-book approach. Still, the importance of such a combination wasn't obvious to everybody. The human relations school rarely, if ever, breathed a word about ownership. Scanlon focused more on gainsharing—a cash bonus—than on equity.

Even some of Louis Kelso's supporters were leery of getting their young movement entangled with workplace involvement schemes. When Corey Rosen started the National Center for Employee Ownership in late 1980, one of the organization's first goals was to find out if ESOPs—then new—really made a difference to a company's performance, and if so, what made some more successful than others. Rosen optimistically assumed that ownership would indeed make a difference and that publicizing that fact would help them grow. He also thought that some form of participative management, such as the quality-of-worklife movement that was then fashionable, might affect how well the ESOP worked. So he wrote a research proposal to study this question and submitted it the Center for Work and Mental Health at the National Institute of Mental Health (NIMH).

Nothing happened for a year. Then NIMH rejected the proposal. Rosen mentioned the rejection to Jeff Gates, who was working for

Russell Long, and Gates mentioned it to his boss. Gates then wrote a letter to NIMH asking what the agency was doing these days on employee ownership. A few weeks later someone from NIMH called Rosen to say, oh, by the way, your grant proposal was not turned down after all; on the contrary, NIMH would pony up $162,000 for a three-year project. Rosen hired a young PhD student, Katherine Klein, to head the project, and proceeded to study forty-five companies with some three thousand seven hundred employees. The researchers found that ESOPs positively affected company performance only under certain conditions. One of those conditions was participative management, which made a great deal of difference. In 1984, Rosen launched another study to test the earlier project's findings. This one found that companies with high-involvement, participatory management schemes grew between 8 percent and 11 percent faster than would otherwise be expected. That study was published in the *Harvard Business Review* and generated a good deal of favorable reaction—except among many nervous ESOP advocates. One consultant went so far as to send a letter to a few hundred clients implying that Rosen and associates were left-wing crazies.

But the tide soon turned. The research was hard to deny. As the new economy flowered, participative or open-book management systems grew more common. The business press began holding up companies such as W. L. Gore & Associates and SRC as exemplars. The ESOP community itself was tightly knit, and ideas about what worked to improve business performance began to spread.

And then there was the power of an example every bit as powerful as that of United Airlines, but positive rather than negative. Southwest Airlines had begun flying in 1971 as an upstart carrier that operated only within the state of Texas and thus was not subject to the regulatory regimen of the Civil Aeronautics Board. Nobody outside the state paid the little airline much mind. But when the industry was deregulated in 1978, Southwest began to grow. And grow. It added cities in other southwestern states. It began flying to other parts of the country. To keep costs low, it flew point-to-point rather than through hubs. It dispensed with frills such as meals and assigned seats. It operated only one kind of aircraft (Boeing 737s), thereby minimizing training and maintenance expenses. With costs substantially below those of the other major airlines, it set fares at seemingly impossible levels. Yet it made money quarter after quarter and year after year.

Southwest was also known for creating a workplace unlike many others, and certainly unlike any other in the contentious airline business. On the one hand, Southwest employees were renowned for their take-no-prisoners discipline. They repeatedly won the "triple crown"— actually an award created by the company rather than one acknowledged by the industry—for best on-time performance, fewest customer complaints, and fewest mishandled bags. They were able to "turn" an airplane—get it unloaded, loaded up again, and back in the air—in about half the time required by other airlines. "Southwest has by far the most productive employees of any major U.S. airline," declared a study by Brandeis University professor Jody Hoffer Gittell.[49] On the other hand, the airline and its employees were also known for creating a zany, relaxed environment. The workplace was more casual than at other airlines. Supervisors toiled alongside frontline employees. The company sponsored plenty of parties. Workers were encouraged to liven things up with practical jokes. (The occasional flight attendant would hide in the overhead luggage bins, waiting to be discovered by the unsuspecting passenger who opened the bin.) Southwest combined this loose employee-centric culture with extensive stock-ownership programs and generous profit sharing. Though nearly all employees were union members, they learned to think and act like the owners they were. They got information that helped them understand how individual contributions (regarding turn time, for example) made a difference. "Southwest doesn't treat front-line people like second-class citizens; it treats them like owners and partners who not only have a right to this information but, more importantly, *need* to know it in order to do their jobs more effectively."[50] They pitched in where needed. "'If we see two strollers off to the side on the tarmac that say CLAIM AT GATE,' says Captain Terry 'Moose' Millard, 'we'll walk down the jetway and get 'em. By the time one of us gets back with the strollers, the ramp agent has thrown twenty or thirty more bags.'"[51]

And then there was the landmark ten-year collective-bargaining agreement, signed by the company and the Southwest Airlines Pilots Association (SWAPA) in 1995. That, you will recall, was the year United's ESOP was doing well. United had recently introduced low-fare "shuttle" operations in California, deliberately designed to compete with Southwest. In 1995, in return for stock options, SWAPA pilots agreed to take no wage increase for the first five years of the new contract, thereby helping to ensure that the carrier's labor costs would remain low. Well before the end of that five-year period, United's unionized pilots were already pushing their employer's costs up. In 2000 they began their slowdown, and their airline was on its way to bankruptcy court. Southwest Airlines—an exemplar of the equity model, precisely because it combined ownership with employee involvement—continued to grow and make money.

Part Three

BUILDING A SUCCESSFUL EQUITY-BASED COMPANY

Taking Ownership Seriously

The remaining chapters of this book will analyze and dissect the equity model. We are leaving the history to focus on how companies are putting the ideas into practice today. A few notes before we begin.

First, we will follow the three-part schema outlined in chapter 2. The equity model consists of (1) sharing ownership, (2) building a culture of ownership, and (3) enabling employees to drive business performance by learning key business disciplines. This chapter looks at ownership itself. Chapter 6 focuses on culture, and chapter 7 on business disciplines. We'll try to show how companies implement each of these three ideas, and we'll describe some of the obstacles they can encounter in the process. Each element is part of the whole and reinforces the other two. A company can implement one at a time, but it won't get the full effect without implementing all three. Yet none of these elements is static, something to be installed and then forgotten about like a new piece of machinery. Building an equity company is very much a dynamic process. People learn from experience. They try out new stuff and see what works. Equity develops over time.

Second, the equity model can't be described in a blueprint. There is no one right way to implement any of its building blocks, hence no one right way to implement the model. There are no Seven Steps to Success. As you will see in the following pages, companies have created dozens of different tools and techniques for making ownership real and for getting employees to think and act like owners. What matters most are the principles. If a particular practice seems to incorporate the principles, it can help build an equity company.

Third, the group of companies that are implementing those principles is broad. It includes long-established corporate giants and recent start-ups, globe-spanning enterprises and small local shops, along with organizations of almost every age and size level in between. The disparity shouldn't faze you. If you work for a large corporation, there is still plenty to learn from how smaller companies go about things, and vice versa. Just as the states are often considered to be "laboratories of democracy" (in Justice Brandeis's words), so small and midsize companies can be seen as laboratories of equity.

As we begin these nuts-and-bolts chapters, it's worth remembering why we're writing about this not-always-simple model of running a company. Taking ownership seriously dramatically changes the basis for collaboration between employees and managers. It gets people committed on a whole new level to the success of the business. It enables companies to do things that they can't otherwise do. It enhances their performance beyond what would otherwise be possible. That is why we propose to go into detail about how companies make the model work. It's worth the time and trouble.

CREATING OWNERSHIP

Ownership is a powerful notion, implying as it does a whole packet of rights and responsibilities. But the word has different meanings in different circumstances, particularly in business. At one extreme, someone who is sole owner of a company gets to determine the direction of the business, hire and fire people at will (almost), and spend the company's money. He or she will also be held personally accountable for delivering goods or services, paying the company's bills, and otherwise living up to commitments made in the firm's name. At the other extreme, someone who owns a few shares in a publicly traded company has no rights except a (generally meaningless) vote for the board and a share in stock appreciation (or losses) and dividends. He or she has no responsibilities for the business. In between are endless permutations and combinations: majority stakes, big minority holdings, preferred stock, common stock, and so on. Any one person's rights and responsibilities as an owner vary depending on the ownership structure of the company—which is to say they vary depending on who else shares ownership and under what circumstances they do so.

Everybody takes these differences for granted, of course, because what ownership means in most contexts is so familiar. But employee ownership is not familiar. When companies make their employees owners, by whatever means, workers usually aren't sure what their ownership entails. Is it more like investor-style ownership of the business, or is it more like sole ownership? Do they now get to decide when and where they will work? Are they entitled to know what the CEO (or their own boss) makes? Are they safe from being laid off or fired? Management itself may not be crystal-clear about its objectives in making employees owners. Maybe the company just wants to give people a little more compensation, in the form of stock rather than cash. (That's essentially what those CEOs who woke up and said, "Let's give everybody one hundred options" were doing.) Maybe it has some vague hope that a few shares of stock will automatically change the way people think and act in the workplace. Expectations on both sides at the beginning tend to be murky and, unless they are clarified, will probably remain so.

So a company that wants to take ownership seriously—a company that wants to pursue the equity model—has a major chore on its hands. It must define what employee ownership means and help everyone in the organization understand it. It must make ownership *real* in any number of ways so that employees run into reminders of their new role wherever they turn. The default hypothesis in any workplace is always business as usual: people are paid to do a job, and their only responsibility is to do it. A company that wants to change the default by expecting people to think and act like owners has to attack it on a variety of fronts. Since the task is hard to imagine in the abstract, we'll examine in some detail how one company goes about it.

SAIC

SAIC, formally known as Science Applications International Corporation, is a company that defies easy description. By its own account it is one of the largest information technology (IT) services firms in the world. It offers systems integration. It provides IT and telecommunications software, a variety of engineering services, and consulting. It does contract research and development, mostly for governmental agencies but also for commercial customers, on subjects ranging from weapons systems and space flight on the one hand to health care and environmental preservation on the other. It runs the National Cancer Institute's research center in Frederick, Maryland. It has operations in forty-eight states and the District of Columbia and in more than twenty-five countries around the world. Nearly three-quarters of SAIC's forty-five thousand employees are professional and technical personnel. Of the thirty-two thousand or so with a college degree, 7 percent hold a doctorate, and 38 percent a master's. The company's financial performance since its founding in 1969 has always been solid and at times has been exceptional. SAIC's revenues and profits have risen every single year since its inception. In fiscal 2004 its sales hit $6.7 billion, up from $5.9 billion the year before. Its net income was $341 million, up from $256 million. In 2004 it ranked 289 on the *Fortune* 500 and appeared on the magazine's list of "Most Admired Companies." It is one of the largest employee-owned firms—and for that matter, one of the largest privately held companies—in the world.

Unlike a lot of big companies, SAIC isn't that old. The company is the creation of a man named J. Robert Beyster, a tall, soft-spoken scientist who is known to his friends as Bob and to many others as Dr. Beyster or just "Dr. B." Beyster earned his bachelor's, master's, and doctoral degrees in engineering and physics from the University of Michigan, served as a lieutenant commander in the navy during World War II, and after the war worked for Westinghouse; the National Scientific Laboratory at Los Alamos, New Mexico; and General Atomic. Back then, he says, he found entrepreneurship "somewhat distasteful"—better that scientists should be working on scientific projects than starting companies. But in 1968 Gulf Oil took over General Atomic and shifted the company's focus. So Beyster and a small group of colleagues left to start a new business. Beyster, the leader, didn't have one big idea; still less did he have a grand plan for the new company. "I was not the brilliant, flash-of-inspiration type of entrepreneur," he says now. "I was more of a persistent, builder type. Rather than having a grand design, we started with some contracts and a few people with ideas, and growth started to snowball."[1]

But Beyster did come up with another kind of big idea, which was that the people who worked for his young company should own it. He figured it was partly a matter of basic fairness: "What happens at most companies is somebody else owns it and you work there. Your labor goes to increase the company's stock price, but you do not share any of the benefits. In an employee-owned company, you get to share in those benefits . . . You not only get paid a fair market value for the skills you bring to SAIC, but your net worth is also increased by the fruits of your efforts." (Joseph Walkush, an executive vice president of SAIC and a longtime Beyster associate, put the same idea a little more bluntly in a recent speech: "We didn't want that other situation where you got a bunch of people over here who are generating profit and doing great work and a bunch of people over there who are getting rich off it.") Beyster can't recall ever hearing Louis Kelso speak, nor did he follow any kind of how-to book. Handing out ownership to the employees just seemed like a "fair way" to structure things. It was also a smart move for a young, scientifically oriented company. Government contracts, which at the time were SAIC's only substantial source of revenue, often went to the leading lights in various fields. Beyster could offer those lights a place to do contractual scientific work largely unhampered by other responsibilities, and he could offer them equity in the company besides. Why wouldn't a scientist sign up? As one old SAIC hand puts it, "It was a heckuva business model."

Thanks to Beyster's commitment to the idea, SAIC today takes employee ownership as seriously as any company in America. The company's literature and Web site identify it as employee owned. (Type "SAIC" into Google, and the first listing is "SAIC—An Employee-Owned Company.") Its annual report devotes many headlines and several pages of text to its philosophy of employee ownership. ("Employee ownership has given us the flexibility to react to our customers' needs in ways other companies cannot.") Behind all this exterior decor is a rather startling infrastructure of staff time and expertise that is devoted to getting stock into employees' hands and to making sure that people understand what it means to be owners.

Karen Garsson, for example, is director of stock programs—"a whole host of programs," as she puts it—which she proceeds to tick off to a visitor. Employees can buy stock outright, for cash, through SAIC's internal market (more on this later). A manager can use stock options as an incentive tool. For example, options might be offered to an employee in a "match to purchase" arrangement in recognition of good performance: the employee buys fifty shares, say, and the company gives her another twenty-five on option. The first-time-buyer program, open to individuals who have never purchased stock in the internal market, also uses options in a match-to-purchase arrangement. First-time buyers may buy up to $2,000 worth of shares; they then get two options from the company for every share they purchase. Managers can recommend stock options or stock itself as a bonus for their employees. ("As a company, we issue stock bonuses to roughly fifteen thousand people, or about a third of the population," says Garsson.) Meanwhile, the company's retirement-plans department offers two ownership plans. One is a direct stock-purchase plan, through which employees can buy shares at a discount for their retirement accounts. The other is the employee stock retirement plan (ESRP), through which the company contributes stock outright to employees' retirement accounts. All told, the people who work for SAIC own roughly 83 percent of their employer—that includes stock held in retirement plans plus shares held directly by current employees—with most of the remaining shares held by former employees. Beyster himself owns roughly 0.4 percent of the shares.

Garsson and several colleagues also run an unusual outfit known as Bull, Inc. A subsidiary of SAIC, Bull, Inc. is a broker-dealer firm registered with the Securities and Exchange Commission (SEC), and Garsson and the rest of its professional staff are licensed brokers. But Bull, Inc. deals only in one stock: its parent company's. Four times a year, typically, it runs a trade, which works essentially as follows. A week before the trade, the company announces the new share price, which it has established with the help of independent financial experts. Employees and other shareholders who want to trade let Bull, Inc. know how much they would like to buy or sell, and at the end of the week Bull, Inc. nets out buyers and sellers to clear the market. If there are too many buyers or too many sellers, the company may step in to make up the difference by issuing new shares or buying up the excess. Perhaps not surprisingly, the balance between buyers and sellers shifts much as it does in other markets. During periods of optimism and regularly rising share prices—much of the 1990s, for example—buyers have outnumbered sellers. In the first years of the new century—a bad time for a lot of markets—the reverse was true.

The sheer quantity of stock-based compensation and the prominence of the quarterly trade help keep employee ownership in the forefront of people's minds. But SAIC also assumes that employees have to *learn* to think of themselves as owners. It publishes materials that are designed, Garsson says, to "really increase the level of understanding and knowledge of employee ownership" among its employees. SAIC's employee owner relations department, which focuses on ownership communications, maintains a series of pages on the company's intranet known as the employee owner's network, or EON. It has also created a so-called certified employee owner (CEO) program comprising a series of online courses. As of early 2004, more than eight thousand of the company's employees had completed the courses, which include titles such as "Introduction to Our Culture and Business," "Introduction to SAIC Operating Financials," and "Stock Options Workshop." It may be a good thing that employees have these educational opportunities, because they might otherwise be swamped with unintelligible information. Quarterly Webcasts—"town hall meetings"—led by senior executives update all employees on the company's business and financial performance. Unit-by-unit summaries of the business are available on the intranet.

Not long ago, the Beyster Institute sponsored a contest for people at employee-owned companies. (The Beyster Institute is a nonprofit organization that is affiliated with the Rady School of Management at the University of California, San Diego, and that helped support the research for this book. As its name suggests, it has close ties to SAIC.) The assignment was to say what employee ownership meant to them. One of the honorable mentions went to Ken Shannon, a senior analyst who had joined SAIC only three months earlier. Shannon's response to the question suggests that the company's efforts along these lines are not wasted:

At SAIC, I have been astonished at the fervor related to employee ownership. The introduction of employee ownership concepts forms a large part of the new employee orientation. There are Web sites dedicated to supporting employee ownership. There are a variety of ways for employees to increase their ownership, including direct purchase of stock and award of stock bonuses.

But the most significant aspect of SAIC's approach to employee ownership is that employees are not just encouraged to act like owners, but we are treated like owners. The amount of information that is made available about the financial operation of the organization is remarkable. This has the effect of not only producing a feeling of confidence in what the future might bring, but also of suggesting that we can influence that future as well. By exposing the financial workings of the company so thoroughly, I become not just a better informed owner but a more effective employee. And this detailed knowledge that I gain about how a company produces profits makes me a better employee and a better owner wherever I might go in the future.[2]

THE KEYS TO REAL OWNERSHIP

SAIC is not a typical employee-owned company. It is larger than most, and its employees are better educated. It reflects its founder's passionate commitment to the concept, maintained since the company's inception. It operates that internal market for buying and selling shares. (To our knowledge, only a few other U.S. companies have comparable internal markets. One is CH2M Hill, an eleven thousand–employee engineering and construction firm based in Englewood, Colorado.) Much more typical of the employee-ownership universe are two other kinds of companies: small to medium-sized businesses that are owned partly or primarily through an ESOP and thus have no provision at all for ongoing trading of shares, and publicly traded companies that hand out stock options or shares to all (or nearly all) of their employees. (Of course, publicly traded companies can and do have ESOPs, and many closely held companies give options to most or all of their employees.) But what's interesting is that wherever employee ownership "works"—wherever employees actually come to think and act like owners, as opposed to regarding the whole thing as just a nice extra benefit—it has several features in common regardless of company size and structure.

Significant Ownership—and Regular Additions

We noted earlier in this book that it matters greatly *how much* stock employees own. Not that they as a group necessarily need to own all or even a majority of shares; Southwest Airlines, for instance, has built a powerful culture of ownership even though its employees own less than 15 percent of the company. But employees need to own enough stock to make a difference in their personal financial situation. Partly this is a matter of common sense. Ownership that doesn't make a difference to your pocketbook isn't likely to matter much in any other way. It's like inheriting a few shares of AT&T from Aunt Tillie—nice, but not a big factor in your overall life situation or financial planning. And partly it's a matter of equity, in the sense of fairness. If your employer expects ownership to make a difference—if it expects you to think and act like an owner, and work accordingly—it should make all that extra effort worth your while. The purpose of a business, after all, is to generate wealth. A proclamation that we're all in this together rings hollow if most employees don't have much wealth at stake. It rings even hollower if top executives, meanwhile, get enough to finance a small country.

As it happens, the common-sense-and-fairness argument is borne out by research dating back to that 1980s study funded by the National Institute of Mental Health and sponsored by the National Center for Employee Ownership. The project's researchers studied all sorts of variables, such as company size, industry, unionization, board representation of employees, and so on, to determine which, if any, had an effect on business performance. They found that participative management made a substantial difference, as we mentioned in the previous chapter. They also found that the *size* of a company's annual contribution to the ESOP mattered a great deal. (Interestingly, contribution size was only somewhat related to participative management, meaning that it had an independent effect on outcomes.) "This," the authors declared, "is a key finding. Employees respond to ownership primarily as a financial incentive . . . The central idea behind early ESOP legislation was to broaden the ownership of wealth; employees appear to endorse the idea."[3] The size of the ESOP contribution didn't simply correlate with business performance; it also affected employee attitudes, as measured by their interest in looking for another job, the attention they paid to company financial results, their willingness to make suggestions and work more efficiently, and so on. In short, the larger the contributions, the more they thought and acted like owners.

Equally important are regular *additions* of stock to employees' portfolios. The United Airlines experiment failed in part because people who were included in the ESOP buyout got all the stock in the first five years that they were ever going to get, and people who joined it later got none at all. The idea of employee ownership became sort of a dead letter, and in fact employees knew it would be so from the time the plan started. By contrast, SAIC contributes, sells, or awards stock to its employees every year. The fact of ownership and the value of the stock are high on the list of what people pay attention to, because they have regular reasons to think about it. Indeed, this may be the answer to the question raised in chapter 3, as to whether options constitute "real" ownership in the same way an ESOP or direct stock ownership does. One-time or occasional awards of options may not feel like real ownership. Employees will sell the shares that the options entitle them to, or they may hold on to them. But they will not have reason to think that ownership will be an important part of their financial future. Starbucks, by contrast, hands out options every January to everyone who has been employed at least six months and who works at least twenty hours per week. The options vest over a five-year period, 20 percent per year. They are a significant part of what the company calls its "total pay" package (referred to as "your special blend" because it is unique to each person). A long-term Starbucks employee would be crazy not to pay attention to his or her ownership in the company, particularly in light of the increase in the stock price over the years. (It increased more than fourfold between 1999 and 2004.)

Substantial and regular contributions of stock generate a kind of buzz among employees. People begin paying attention to the stock value. They gossip about each other's accounts. Everyone knows about the "Microsoft millionaires"—but you don't need the explosive growth of a Microsoft to generate seven-figure account balances. Over the years, estimates a veteran SAIC employee named Bill Scott, SAIC has created some three thousand millionaires through sharing ownership. (At both companies, one challenge facing managers is that some of their employees no longer have to work and will do so only as long as their jobs are challenging and interesting. Of course, the same could be said of most CEOs, though nobody seems to worry about that.) In smaller companies, six-figure balances may be equally common and as frequently talked about over the water cooler. For example:

- McKay Nursery Company is a small company in Waterloo, Wisconsin. Its annual sales are in the neighborhood of $14 million. But it is 100 percent owned by its employees and has been since 1984, giving people time to accumulate sizable balances. "A full-time employee that has been here twenty-some years, they're probably going to have three-quarters of a million dollars [in their account]," says chief financial officer Tim Jonas. "And they didn't put a nickel into it." McKay relies heavily on seasonal laborers, mainly Mexicans and Mexican Americans who work from March until November and who earn perhaps $28,000 in wages in the several months they are with McKay. The company includes them in the ESOP, and one seasonal worker who recently retired had built up a stock balance of $150,000. Needless to say, most of these employees return year after year.

- Phelps County Bank, in Rolla, Missouri, is also wholly owned by its employees. It too has had an ESOP for many years, and despite its small-town location has been remarkably successful. As of 2003, employees' *average* account balance was about $300,000— and that included some newer employees who hadn't had much time to build up their accounts. The bank allows individuals with so many years of service to withdraw certain amounts from their ESOP accounts. Wendy Young, a loan officer, was exploring in vitro fertilization with her husband, but found that it was expensive. Fortunately, she was eligible to withdraw $5,000 from her ESOP account at the time—enough, she reports, for "one shot at in vitro." It worked: "We got lucky and had twins. We would not have been able to do that without the ESOP."

Such stories percolate throughout a company. But then, ownership tends to resonate day in and day out with business performance, just as it does for any company owner. When an employee-owned company is doing well, the effect is almost tangible, precisely because of the employees' financial stake. W. L. Gore & Associates sales rep John Czerwinski says,

> Right now you can almost feel it, walking around the halls—
> even though our five-year compounded growth rate isn't any-
> thing like the hooplas of the '90s. We're not in the 20 percent
> five-year rate. But it's positive, and even more so it's trending
> upward, and we have a lot of things in the pipeline, and so
> right now everybody's feeling a lot of ownership. There's really
> something here. We can really make this happen—let's get be-
> hind it and go.

Gore typically contributes stock worth 12 percent of an associate's salary every year to that person's ESOP account and another 3 percent to his or her 401(k) plan. Adds Czerwinski, "You don't need to have double-digit growth to get rich when you're banking 15 percent of your salary"—particularly since that 15 percent is *in addition to* the employee's full salary, not deducted from it.

Ownership Education

Most companies of any size have a training budget. Like SAIC, equity companies typically spend part of that budget helping their employees learn about both *ownership* and *business*. The two are necessarily intertwined. Understanding ownership means understanding the rights and responsibilities that go along with it, to be sure. But it also entails understanding how the business operates. People with high school educations—and many with college degrees—don't learn much about business in school. Ask someone on the street to explain the difference between debt and equity, how net income is different from net cash, or what it means to increase inventory turns, and you're likely to draw a blank stare. But it is precisely such matters that the employees of equity companies need to learn, and do learn, through both formal and informal training.

Companies naturally pursue differing strategies. Green Mountain Coffee Roasters' training program, mentioned in chapter 2, put every employee through a seven-and-a-half-hour course (spread over three days) shortly after the company instituted its ESOP. Building Materials Distributors, Inc. (BMD), a $100 million–plus wholesaler and exporter of building materials headquartered in Galt, California, takes a different approach: it runs intensive classes for small groups of employees, who are then expected to share their knowledge with their peers. Individuals at BMD are nominated to attend the program, which includes twenty classes over a two-year period. They learn to understand the company's financials and key business drivers, how the ESOP works and how the business is valued, how to understand the operating statements, and so on. When they complete the courses, they are named certified employee owners, as at SAIC, and receive $500 in cash, along with miscellaneous awards such as shirts and bags. "We've had drivers, outside salespeople, and accountants [go through the training]," says Steve Ellinwood, the company's president. "They're our spokespeople. They meet with our board members and trustees."

At Cisco Systems, where ownership is a key driver of the culture, all employees worldwide get options regularly; they also can (and most do) buy stock at a discount through Cisco's employee stock purchase plan (ESPP). Given its global scale, Cisco can't hold the kind of employee educational meetings smaller companies can, but its employees are accustomed to using the Web to gather information. Thus, for instance, Cisco employees can go to an elaborate intranet page and click on "MyStockInfo," which is automatically customized for each employee. The site gives them details about their options grants and ESPP participation and allows them access to plan documents, frequently asked questions, discussions of financial planning strategies, and other information. Cisco also uses its intranet for regular presentations about its financial performance and for a large variety of educational programs on the company, its financials, and general business and technology issues.

Cisco employees engage with the company around issues of ownership. One employee, for instance, learned that under an ESPP, employees are given the right to buy stock at a 15 percent discount off its price at any point up to twenty-seven months in the past, provided only that they have been setting aside payroll funds for that long to buy shares. Cisco had only a six-month "look back" feature. So the employee sent an e-mail to CEO John Chambers, who changed the program to a two-year look-back. Another employee created a Web page when a colleague exercised options to buy a new car. The employee thought the colleague should have held on to the options longer to let their value increase more than it already had. So he put a picture of the car on the Web, with the price paid for it, and how much the car "cost" the employee in terms of forgone options gains. Cisco's HR department couldn't have designed a more powerful communications tool.

Much of the ownership education done by equity companies is informal. It's a combination of on-the-job instruction and ad hoc educational experiences ("teachable moments," as pedagogues put it). Employees of Stone Construction Equipment learn to understand labor variances because the figures are tracked and reported to them every day. Gardener's Supply, the Vermont-based catalog retailer, holds a "guess the share price" contest just before the company's annual valuation, and recently conducted an exercise in which employees were asked to list the company's top twenty costs. (That, in turn, led to a discussion of how to save money on the biggest items.) Thoits Insurance Service, Inc., in Mountain View, California, makes a game out of teaching and learning about its ESOP and hence about ownership. "We have worked hard to make education fun," says HR director Karen Aasen, who ticks off the game-show-style educational exercises the company has set up. "We have ESOP Bingo. We've played Scattergories using ESOP terminology. We have ESOP Wheel of Fortune—we've used that game for the past six years to help familiarize people with ESOP terms. In the past, we've played ESOP Squares—like Hollywood Squares—and Jeopardy."

What's distinctive about ownership education as compared with the usual training that companies provide is its emphasis on the big picture and hence on concepts that are usually foreign to frontline employees and supervisors, and on the *line of sight* between what employees do every day and the company's business results. Brian Jones is chief executive officer of Nypro, Inc., an eleven thousand–employee global manufacturer of plastic injection-molded products that is headquartered in

Clinton, Massachusetts. Nypro always had an employee-oriented culture and a profit-sharing plan, but only in 1998 did it establish an ESOP to buy the retiring founder's stock. Jones describes how the company's already well-developed on-the-job education had to change focus:

> For over thirty years we've had a profit-sharing system that all of the employees share. It's driven off a daily report. That daily report lists every job for every customer, every machine, every plant, and tells you at the bottom of the report, based on how you operated today, what would be the profit for every single job, and for the plant, and what the profit sharing would be at the end of the quarter. So [employees] have a direct connection [between] what they're going to get in a check based on whether they do better than they did today or they do worse. Whether they solve problems on the machines and jobs or whether they don't . . . It's all based on controllable costs. We exclude any tax items, depreciation items, and changes in accounting standards. We exclude SG&A totally.[4] [It includes] materials, direct labor, indirect labor, efficiency of the machine cells, quality of the machine cells. It compares the actual to the standard, which was the quote. Every employee sees it! Most companies, you can work twenty years on a machine and you never know what value is created. What the costs were. Whether it was over or under. You certainly could never make a connection between what your profit sharing might be based on how that machine ran.
>
> So going from that system to an ESOP system was not a huge leap of faith. We have shared $63 million through profit sharing over the last thirty years. That's a lot of money. So that obviously tells you what the fundamental idea is about the involvement of the employees in creating success. In other words, management doesn't think they do it alone . . . [Still,] the daily report is based on a particular job, making a particular part. When you go to an ESOP, employees are looking at company statements on valuation [because] there's an external valuation done. People knew nothing about valuation or the balance sheet. They didn't know how to read an income statement . . . [So now] we're trying to

connect valuation, which is driven off of various things—growth rates, profit, EBITDA—they didn't know what EBITDA was; nobody in this company knew what EBITDA was! They had never used EBITDA before. So you had to explain what EBITDA was, how to calculate it, what it's driven from.[5] And inventory! They didn't know anything about inventory. They'd never looked at inventory. Inventory was something you had to have. When a customer wants parts, you have to have inventory. Well, no. They never saw inventory as cash. And this has a lot to do with the valuation . . .

So we actually created a series of communications in the first year leading up to the ESOP. And then in the first year there were a lot of intense communications that tied these different things into their actual dollars in the [ESOP] trust. The shares that were allocated and the value of those shares. We had to create a direct connection between these things and their stock value. Just like we did with their daily report, how the job runs and their profit sharing, we tried to create the same direct line of sight between the factors that set the valuation and their actual stock. So, for instance, we would say, if inventory goes down from thirty days to twenty-eight days, two days improvement in inventory, we'd dollarize that. We said, that would lead to a $7 increase in your stock price . . . If our cash requirements go down by 10 percent, the stock is going to go up by $12. If scrap rates change by this much, it's going to affect the stock. So basically we tried to create a direct link between these factors that are in the valuation and the outcomes in the stock. This is obviously a learning drill.

So it's a challenge. But it's actually worked out pretty well.

Information

The idea of all this education, of course, is to help employees understand what is going on in the business so they can act like the owners they are. A corollary requirement is that people need to have regular, ongoing information about the state of things. Equity companies seem to take this requirement almost for granted. SAIC has its quarterly Webcast and regular business-unit meetings. Nypro makes a point of sending its executives to every location and every shift to brief employ-ees on the state of the business once a quarter. Smaller companies get together more often. For example:

- At BMD, managers meet monthly to review the state of the busi-ness and are then expected to share the information in staff meet-ings with their direct reports. Employees as a group meet quarterly to hear business and financial updates from company president Ellinwood. Also quarterly, the company buys dinner for ware-house employees, who then get a chance to pose questions to se-nior managers. Every week, a senior manager takes a group of five employees representing different departments out to lunch, giving them a chance to talk about the business informally. Every six months, employees meet as shareholders with the ESOP trustees and the company's board of directors.

- Phelps County Bank holds bimonthly "ownership" meetings. "We bring all employees in collectively, and we talk about every single thing that's going on in the bank," says CEO Bill Marshall. "We go over all of our growth patterns, where we are on the budget. We go through all the details—how much money we're spending, how that's going to affect the bottom line, what it's going to do to the ESOP. So they're all intimately involved in knowing exactly what we're trying to do all the time." These bimonthly gatherings are supplemented with regular departmental meetings. "Just about every single department in the bank, at least on a weekly basis, we have different meetings that go on," adds Marshall. "At those meet-ings, we talk about our balance sheet, our income statements, where we are in different areas."

- Scot Forge holds monthly meetings over lunch, which is bought by the company. Accountant Karen York describes what happens: "After we eat, different people talk. The top managers talk about our financials, our operations for the month that we just closed, how we're doing on our profit sharing, all that stuff. We talk about what's going on in the shop, what we're buying new, what we're rebuilding, what we're replacing, any problems we're having. We talk about quality a lot. That is a big cost area. It's an area where

it's really easy to save money, if we're really careful about the quality of the product going out . . . Just everybody being there in that
room, shop people, office people, officers, everybody sitting there,
just being together and [listening] to the same message. I think
that helps a lot to make people feel like they're really involved and
they're really part of it."

- At Herman Miller, Inc., a publicly traded furniture manufacturer
  with widespread employee ownership, the key performance driver
  is economic value added (EVA), a measure of a business's after-tax
  cash flow less the cost of capital the company employs. Satisfactory EVA performance triggers payments to both a cash bonus
  pool and a deferred profit-sharing plan. All employees take classes
  on EVA; each work unit develops critical number targets based on
  maximizing their contributions to EVA; EVA "driver trees" show
  the impact of particular work units on overall measurements; and
  employees meet in monthly groups to discuss results. A quarterly
  video sent to each team provides background data by reviewing a
  detailed series of varying financial data, such as backlog, gross
  margin, and materials costs changes, with an explanation of why
  changes have occurred.

Meetings, of course, are only one means of sharing information.
SAIC posts immense quantities of information on its internal Web site.
BMD puts something called the "daily news" on its intranet and on
bulletin boards around the company; the sheet includes sales and
profitability compared with budget as well as the usual round of
announcements. Gardener's Supply distributes an "ESOP report" each
month to every employee; the report includes the company's financial
data. In the information age, it isn't hard for companies to figure out
how to get the word out. What's distinctive about equity companies is
that they think it is important to do so. Sharing information in this
manner accomplishes at least three objectives. It makes people feel a
part of the company. It gives them the information they need to make
more—and better—decisions in their jobs. It also turns everyday business into a kind of game. We'll discuss this notion later in the book; for
now, it's enough to say that "keeping score" in this way makes work that
much more interesting.

The Magic of the Multiple (and Other Ownership Rewards)

Ownership teaches employees the great secret of capitalism, just as Louis Kelso might have hoped. Call it the magic of the multiple: if you increase the earnings of a company you own by $1, then the value of the business increases by $5 or $10 or $20—whatever the price-to-earnings ratio may be. (Even closely held companies have an implicit price-to-earnings ratio, because the value of the company varies with its profits.) As an owner of the business, your net worth rises accordingly. This is what Brian Jones of Nypro was referring to when he helped people understand the connection between increasing profits and boosting the value of employees' ESOP accounts. According to Phelps County Bank CEO Bill Marshall, it is one factor that motivates the bank's employees to deliver good service. "They understand that banks are valued between thirteen and fifteen times earnings. So they know that every dollar that comes into this bank in the form of income turns into $15 in the form of ESOP. A dollar's worth of income is worth fifteen on the other side. Every transaction, every single relationship with a customer benefits the employees directly. So they go much, much further than maybe an average employee would." The magic of the multiple, of course, is the way people accumulate substantial wealth through ownership.

But when employees own part or all of a company, they are also entitled to whatever the board of directors may decide to pay the share owners by way of dividends. Some companies explicitly call these payments dividends and treat them as such. Others instead pay employee owners generous amounts in profit sharing, to avoid the double taxation of dividends. But it scarcely matters how the money is handled and accounted for: in either case the employees, as owners, gain both from the increased value of the company and from whatever cash the board and senior executives may decide to pay out now.

Because of this, equity companies are often startlingly generous in the total compensation they offer their people. Hypertherm, a Hanover, New Hampshire, manufacturer of plasma cutting machines for metalworking industries, has paid out profit sharing in recent years that averaged 28 percent of base wages—roughly an additional three months' pay per person. McKay Nursery pays a cash bonus that varies between

10 percent and 50 percent of wages. "The cash bonus helps to really re-inforce ownership," says CFO Tim Jonas. "People understand that if the company as a whole makes more money, the likelihood of them mak-ing more money is going to be greater, and vice versa." McKay also pays a separate cash bonus that varies with the number of shares an em-ployee owns. Scot Forge pays its employee owners both profit sharing and dividends on their stock; a five-year employee averages 10 percent of salary in profit sharing, for example, and a fifteen-year employee will average another 12 percent of salary in dividends. "We get those checks twice a year," says Leo Szlembarski, a lathe operator. "Right? It's great! Two thousand, three thousand, four thousand. That's a lot of money. Those checks are educating my kids."

Just as such payments reinforce the message of ownership, they also reinforce the benefits that the equity model creates for both employer and employee. People line up at the door to work at such companies. Once in, they are eager to stay.

THE CHALLENGES OF OWNERSHIP

We said earlier in this book that the equity model as a whole is de-manding of employees and that it can be hard to implement. Those are two reasons why it is not more widespread. Even the ownership com-ponent alone can pose a range of difficulties, both for employees them-selves and for a company's managers.

Employees start off with all that uncertainty about the rights and responsibilities of ownership mentioned at the beginning of this chap-ter. We're owners! Does it mean we can give ourselves a raise? The sim-plest questions are usually answered quickly; still, employee-owned companies occasionally report that people continue to make overly op-timistic assumptions about their rights as an owner. John Mock, direc-tor of human resources at six-hundred-employee Travel and Transport, a travel-management firm based in Omaha, Nebraska, says that some employees had their noses out of joint because they weren't consulted about a change in health insurance. "Some just said, 'Wait, I'm an owner, why wasn't I brought into the discussion?' Well, instead of ask-ing each and every employee owner what his or her personal thoughts were on the matter, we put it to a specific committee. [My answer was,] 'Hey, we have a committee, and we made a decision.'"

Employees may also mistrust the rhetoric of ownership, particularly if a company has a legacy of labor-management animosity. What are we giving up to get this stock? Nobody gets something for nothing. And how secure is it? Will the company really give people the money that they have accumulated when they retire? Do I really want to have all my retirement eggs in one basket? If a company's stock falls in value, the drop can come as a shock, and suddenly employee ownership can lose some of its allure. "Through the late '90s, when things were kind of cresting and trending down," says Gore's Czerwinski, "you got a little bit more apathy." Educational programs of the sort described earlier in the chapter help to address such issues, but experience is a powerful teacher as well. Companies with ESOPs, for instance, typically also offer 401(k) plans, precisely so that employees will have some diversification in their retirement portfolios. (Also, federal regulations require companies to offer diversification options for ESOP members who reach a certain combination of age and years of service.) They often make a show of paying off retiring employees, just to underscore the fact that the stock accounts represent real money. They make a game out of watching the stock value and comparing it to the market, thus helping people understand that shares can drop in value, to be sure, but that if the company performs well, they almost always rise again. Companies that hand out options to a broad group of employees learned that options may seem less attractive when stock prices fall sharply, as they did a few years ago. For some companies, like Cisco, the answer to this problem was to keep giving out options regularly, helping employees understand that some of their grants will probably always be "under water," while others will be granted at closer to the bottom of the stock price cycle and will be quite valuable. Other companies, such as Microsoft, switched to restricted stock, a form of equity grant that ensures employees get some value even if the stock price goes down. However equity is shared, the longer a company operates under employee ownership, the fewer questions arise. But they may never disappear altogether.

Employee ownership also raises several legal and financial issues. Because of the Wagner Act's prohibition against company unions, a company cannot consult with a nonunionized group of employees about wages and benefits—even if those employees are owners of the business. Because of SEC regulations, a publicly traded company can't communicate consolidated financial information to non-"insider" employees before releasing that information to the public. Because of the tax benefits involved, companies that set up ESOPs must comply with a host of legal and accounting requirements. The expense is generally prohibitive for companies with less than $1 million or so in annual payroll, so many small companies interested in employee ownership seek out alternative mechanisms, such as a co-op structure or simply sharing stock directly. This is a legacy of the fact that Russell Long used tax law to encourage employee ownership. But certain kinds of stock options, too, require compliance with complex tax laws. Financially, a closely held company with an ESOP incurs what's known as the repurchase obligation—that is, an obligation to buy back the stock of a retiring employee. If the company is growing and the stock has increased substantially in value, the potential drain on a company's cash is significant. Management must ensure that it has the requisite amounts of cash available.[6]

One of the chief difficulties of successful employee ownership, ironically, is that it can generate prodigious amounts of money for people who happen to be in the right place at the right time. Everyone has heard stories of those Microsoft millionaires or dot-com winners—people who accumulated enough stock or options at a young age that they could simply quit working. But a company doesn't have to win a high-tech lottery to be in this situation; similar problems can arise in any successful company with extensive employee ownership. Take Phelps County Bank, which wouldn't fit anyone's description of a glitzy go-go enterprise. "Because our [ESOP] account balances continued to grow, we ran into a little bit of a dilemma," recalls CEO Marshall. "We had people who were tellers who had been here fifteen years and had $250,000 in their ESOP account. They were saying, 'You know what? With $250,000 I can go home.' So we were having people considering leaving the bank, to take their balances." Phelps County Bank amended its plan to establish two requirements for retirement with an immediate payout: an employee needed at least ten years of service, and his or her age plus years of service had to equal at least sixty. (The balances of those who didn't meet the requirement would be held in an interest-bearing account for five years.) It also amended the plan to allow for "in-service withdrawals" of up to 5 percent of an employee's vested balance each year; again, only employees with a minimum number of years of service were eligible. But even when such restrictions are in place, the logic of a company's growth may create imbalances. Scot Forge, for example, went through a period of rapid expansion not long after the company's ESOP bought out a retiring owner. People on the payroll at the time saw their account balances skyrocket. Those who have been hired more recently have not accumulated as much stock, and the share price has not been rising as quickly. So their accounts are considerably smaller than those of their longer-working peers. A few Scot employees suggested to us that the imbalances "might" create a little resentment. How widespread it might be is hard to estimate.

Finally, there is one aspect of ownership that might seem like a problem but typically turns out not to be. We're referring to the fact that shareholders choose the company's board of directors. In publicly traded companies, of course, there isn't much of an issue; employees who are shareholders get the vote automatically, and their votes count as much—or as little—as those of any other shareholder. If employees have stock options, they almost never have a vote, whether the company is public or not, until they exercise the options, and then, of course, only for as long as they hold on to the shares. But an issue does arise in closely held companies that are largely or wholly owned by an ESOP. Whether employee owners should vote for directors—or whether, by contrast, all the ESOP shares should be voted by the ESOP trustee (who is typically a company senior executive or an outside institution)—has historically been a bone of contention. The law allows an ESOP to be structured either way, and in fact slightly fewer than one-quarter of ESOP companies pass the vote through to employees. But in practice, it doesn't make much difference whether they do or they don't. Boards of directors aren't like town councils. Their members are chosen not as representatives of constituents, but as experts who are qualified to oversee a business. Employees understand this and tend to elect the same people that managers or other shareholders would elect. The fear that employee owners would somehow engineer a coup, or would fill the board seats with underqualified frontline workers, has no basis in fact.

So what can we conclude from this chapter? One conclusion is that changing the ownership of a business—moving from conventional investor or entrepreneurial ownership to some form of employee ownership—is no small matter. It alters people's expectations. It raises issues that simply don't crop up in a conventional business. It presents companies with specific managerial challenges. But a second conclusion is that none of these challenges is insuperable. In fact, all sorts of companies have learned or devised ways of clarifying expectations and of helping employees to see themselves as owners. The payoffs for the employees can be rather substantial. The payoffs for the companies, in higher productivity and lower turnover, can be rather substantial as well. But ownership alone, as we have seen, isn't enough. Companies must also learn to create a different kind of workplace and to run the business in a different way. We will take up these topics in the next two chapters.

6

A Different Kind of Workplace

Just as SAIC enjoys iconic status in the employee-ownership community, W. L. Gore & Associates has become a benchmark and reference point in what might loosely be called the annals of corporate culture. One reason is that Gore is indisputably different from other companies in the way it runs its business. Another may be that the closely held company plays its cards close to the vest. It allows researchers and reporters periodic glimpses of its unusual workplaces—enough to pique anybody's curiosity—but to date it has given no one unlimited access, of the sort that would permit a definitive book or article series on the company's work environment. Like Kremlinologists in the days of the Soviet Union, outside analysts must therefore stitch together a coherent picture of how Gore operates. Still, the picture that can be assembled is compelling enough. Over the years, Gore has challenged most of the conventional organization's chain-of-command assumptions. It illustrates a fundamental principle of our model, which is that an equity company needs to create a different kind of workplace—a workplace in which the fundamental precepts of business-as-usual are very much not taken for granted, and in which the message of ownership is reinforced every day in a dozen different ways.

Wilbert L. Gore himself, known as Bill, was an unlikely managerial revolutionary. A research chemist who worked for DuPont, he grew

interested in the potential of a DuPont material called polytetrafluo-
roethylene (PTFE), better known as the original form of Teflon. In
particular—and inspired by a suggestion from his son Bob, then a
sophomore at the University of Delaware—Gore thought PTFE might
be useful for insulating electrical wires and cables. DuPont wasn't interested in that application, so Bill and his wife, Genevieve, known as
Vieve, started their own company. By 1960, two years after its founding, W. L. Gore & Associates had received its first major order: 7.5
miles of insulated ribbon cable for the city of Denver. Soon Gore was
a thriving little business, with two plants in the United States and a
handful of overseas operations. Gore wires and cables were incorporated into NASA spacecraft, thereby finding their way to the moon.

But the company's big breakthrough came in 1969, when Bob Gore
discovered that PTFE could be stretched, or "expanded." Until then, experimenters trying to heat and stretch the material had always found
that it just broke. But Bob learned that if he heated it rapidly, rather
than in increments, the material could be stretched like taffy without
breaking.[1] The expanded material, known technically as ePTFE but
promptly christened with the Gore-Tex brand, turned out to be the
basis for a dazzling array of new products. It was used for high-speed
cables in mainframes and supercomputers. It was incorporated into
industrial sealants and filter bags. It could also be engineered into a
fabric possessing the unique properties of being at once breathable—
air molecules could pass through it—and waterproof. The 1977
Early Winters catalog advertised its Gore-Tex outerwear, brand new at
the time, as "possibly the most versatile piece of clothing you'll ever
wear."[2] Since then, of course, Gore-Tex fabric has become a popular
and widely used component in many kinds of outdoor clothing and
footwear. It has also been adapted for use in dozens of other markets,
ranging from medical implants to guitar strings. W. L. Gore & Associates at this writing has more than seven thousand employees—yes,
they are known as associates, and if you say "employees" at Gore, you're
likely to be corrected—and about $1.5 billion in annual revenues. It
has operations in forty-five countries around the world, including
manufacturing facilities in the United States, Germany, Scotland,
Japan, and China. Though the company won't reveal earnings, *Fortune*
magazine reported in late 2003 that it "has managed to post a profit

every single year since its founding 45 years ago."[3] In December 2004 it was named by *Fast Company* magazine as the most innovative company in America.

Bill Gore always encouraged scientifically minded associates to dabble in research projects, in hopes that they would create new products. Bill and Vieve themselves dabbled in alternative ways of running a company. They created what Bill liked to call a "lattice" organization, one ostensibly without formal chains of command or channels of communication. They did away not only with the term *employee* but with *supervisor*. They decreed that leaders in the organization (never *managers*) would not necessarily be designated from above, but instead would emerge over time as some people persuaded others to join them in a project. To facilitate face-to-face interaction, the company would keep its plants small, no more than 150 to 200 people. Associates would govern themselves through principles of fairness, individual commitment, consultative or consensual decision making, and "freedom to encourage, help, and allow other associates to grow in knowledge, skill, and scope of responsibility."[4] The ideas were at once intriguing and frustratingly vague. But however murky they might sound to outsiders, they seemed to work. W. L. Gore & Associates grew and prospered. It earned a reputation as a world-class innovator. Employee satisfaction seemed to be off the charts. ("It's in the 85 to 90 percent range," says one senior leader.) The company made the original list of "100 Best Companies to Work For," which was published in book form in 1984, and again when the book was revised and reissued in 1985 and 1993. It has made the annual list every single year since *Fortune* began publishing it in 1998.

When the company was young, Bill Gore and his family, along with a few friends, owned all of the stock. A man named Burt Chase, a high school and college friend of Bob Gore's, had joined the business in 1961, and right away decided he wanted to buy equity in the company. So the Gores sold him some, a share at a time. As the company grew, the stock grew more valuable, and other employees began clamoring for shares. Bill called Chase in, as Chase remembers it, and said, "I've got a list of people who have requested stock. You just got a share, so you're going to the bottom of the list. When you work your way up, I'll call you." In 1974 Gore started an employee stock ownership plan, which is known at the company as the ASOP ("A" for associate). That, says Chase, "solved the problem for all of us. And it was very consistent with Bill Gore's philosophy. We're all citizens . . . Sure, some people own more stock than other people. Some people have more money than other people. But we're all working for the success of the enterprise, which will make us all happy, hopefully, and take care of our financial needs. And that's pretty much what happened."

GORE TODAY

One of us (John Case) had a chance to sit down with several Gore associates for a day's worth of interviews not long ago. (This was one of those periodic glimpses that the company offers outsiders.) The picture of the company that emerged was as remarkable as ever. Today's associates are very much aware and appreciative of Gore's differences and of the difference that its culture makes in their lives. Yet most have been living with the differences long enough to take them for granted and to realize that not everything necessarily works exactly as Bill Gore, who died in 1986, would have liked. ("This is not Nirvana," declared one associate firmly.) They don't give away any of the family secrets, nor do they invite a visitor into any of their plants. But they talk candidly, almost matter-of-factly, about the many small ways in which Gore has created its unusual workplaces.

For starters, there's that matter of language, and it isn't just associates instead of employees or leaders instead of managers. For many years Gore made a point of not giving people job titles—a reflection, explains manufacturing leader Jim Buckley, of the company's emphasis on face-to-face communication in small facilities. "We don't have to have titles, because I know what you do. I know you personally." In any other company Buckley's responsibilities would earn him a title like vice president for global manufacturing. His Gore business card simply says "associate." But recently, some people have begun putting titles on their cards, the Gore folks hasten to add—"titles they make up," mainly for use outside the company. Whether they should or not seems to be a point of mild good-natured debate. But the conversation itself serves to remind everyone that titles may not be as important as the outside world would like them to be.

Different language matters precisely because it challenges unspoken assumptions. So it is with bureaucratic procedures. At virtually every other company in the United States, an employee who wants to be reimbursed for expenses prepares an expense report and gets it signed by a supervisor or department head (sometimes more than one). Gore associates file an "investment report," the very name of which challenges the idea that people are somehow entitled to whatever expenses are in the budget. "The notion is, you should *think* about how you spend the company's money," says Ed Schneider, who works in corporate communications. "It's everybody's money! . . . So you say, OK, how am I spending my time, what am I directing this investment toward, how is it going to benefit what I do, how is it going to benefit the enterprise?" *Nobody* has to approve the form; the associate submits it and is reimbursed. If other associates want to look it up in the database and see what you did last week and how much of their money you spent, they can.

The differences in Gore's plants and offices are substantive as well as semantic—the place really does run differently. For example:

- Every associate at Gore has a *sponsor*. "You have a starting sponsor when you first begin at Gore," explains Burt Chase. "That's an assigned person, in your specific area of responsibility, that you're starting to work with. To help you get started." After a while, people are free to choose their own sponsors. "You get a sense of maybe, gee whiz, this is the guy I have an affinity with, it seems like he's got more stuff to teach me—'Hey, Fred, would you be my sponsor?'" The sponsor serves as mentor, coach, and advocate, but he or she is not in any way an individual's boss. (Gore people wouldn't like the term *boss*, but the point is that the sponsor is not the same person who leads the individual's work group.) Sponsorship is an essential element of the lattice. Nobody gets pigeonholed in a particular work group. Communication takes place informally, across departments.

- Pay at Gore is determined partly by a procedure known as the *contribution ranking*. Once a year, everyone on a work team or project team lists his or her associates in order of the value they are thought to bring to the job, whether through skills, effort, teamwork, or any other trait. The idea came straight from Bill Gore. "He was not in favor of saying, oh, this is a manufacturing company, pay all the extruder operators the same," says Buckley. "He'd say, 'No, that's not fair to the group. There are always a couple, three people who are going to be extraordinary—why wouldn't we be looking at them differently?' So all the people have input. If I were a member of that team, I'd exclude my name, but I'd rank everybody else. If you were a member of the team, you'd do the same." The pay recommendations that emerge from this process are reviewed in six months, more frequently if the group includes a lot of new people.

- *Leaders* at Gore are made, not born. "We pretty much don't hire in leaders," says Buckley, "which is a troublesome thing for some folks." Instead, the company hires people it hopes will become leaders, and watches what they do. If they come up with good ideas, persuade others to adopt those ideas, and regularly turn up toward the top of the contribution rankings, they are likely to find themselves in a leadership role. Not that their new role will necessarily carry much decision-making power. "This is where some people who have been leaders outside the company have difficulty coming in. [The attitude] 'I'm used to making the decisions, doing what I think is best'—that's a hard sell at Gore. A *hard* sell. That person's going to have some problems." John Dennison, who leads an IT team, confirms the importance of not dictating decisions. "In my group there really haven't been situations where we had irreconcilable differences, where I had to come down on one side or the other. But were it to come to that, that's where you step back and ask for some other input, additional associates outside the team to help resolve areas that you haven't gotten to work."

Many decisions indeed, rest with the teams themselves. Plant teams get involved in hiring. They determine their own work schedules. "The building I'm in, we have eight businesses, and I'll bet we have five different starting times," says Robert McCracken, a leader in Gore's "two-millimeter" business unit, which supplies cables and assemblies to the server market and telecommunications industries. "It's whatever works best for that team." In order to make intelligent decisions, of course, teams need information—and they seem to get plenty, mostly through regular shop-floor meetings that review financial performance and other key issues. Team members are also encouraged to come up with ideas for improvement. "People are always trying to think about, 'Today we got 100 units out; tomorrow how can we get 105?'" says McCracken.

> We actually have an idea database on Lotus Notes where they can suggest an idea. And it goes to the manufacturing operations leader, and those two people have a dialogue about it: "Tell me more what you're thinking." . . . [Then] you say, "OK, this is your business, you own a piece of it. Would you cut a check for $25,000 for that microscope or that other piece of equipment?" You talk through how long is this opportunity going to last, how long are you going to utilize the equipment, are you going to get a return on your investment? We talk about the profit share, about the ASOP . . . Money that you don't spend is money that is there at the end of the month for ASOP and for profit sharing.
>
> You have that conversation, and then you figure out what would we have to do to implement it. If we implemented this, could we get 105 instead of 100, every shift, every day, fifty-two weeks a year? And then we tally our return on investment for all the ideas, by the quarter and by the year.

Perhaps because of such involvement, Gore has noticed an interesting phenomenon: when the company conducts a survey asking associates if they consider themselves leaders in the company, fully half of the entire workforce reply that they do. "Now you have to go back and ask people, how did you define 'leader'?" says Buckley. "And you'll get responses like, 'Well, it's because I had input into [a decision]. I helped make it. So I'm providing some leadership.'" One person who might describe himself as a leader is John Czerwinski, the sales rep. Early in his career at Gore, Czerwinski was asked if he'd like to be an ASOP representative, which essentially meant attending meetings about the ASOP and answering questions about the program from fellow associates. Czerwinski especially liked attending the explanations of the company's quarterly stock valuations—"It's like sitting in on a board of directors meeting"—and on his own initiative began reading his notes about the meeting over the company's telecommunications system to his colleagues in sales. In the late '90s somebody came up with the idea that the whole company should hear his broadcasts. That was fine with Czerwinski: "I just picked up the ball and ran with it." Today he and another associate are responsible for letting everyone else in the company know what the stock is valued at and why.

CREATING A CULTURE OF OWNERSHIP

Corporate culture comprises the entire set of beliefs, values, and expectations that govern how people behave in the workplace. It is created through social artifacts—words, practices, procedures, rituals, and so on. But what's important isn't a particular set of artifacts, which in any event vary widely from one company to another. What's important are the cultural messages a company sends to the people who work for it. Conventional companies, as we have noted, are organized so that one group of people performs the work required to generate income and create wealth, while a separate group of people holds ownership rights to that wealth and income. This structure profoundly affects what a company can expect from employees in the way of attitudes and behaviors. In the conventional "hired help" workplace, employees (and many managers) recognize that the workforce is there only, or primarily, as a means to achieve someone else's end. Not surprisingly, management at such a company communicates a series of implicit messages that add up to *We do business here in the ordinary way*. Employees will be expected to show up for work, do their job, and stay out of trouble. Decisions will be made by the chain of command. Information will be disseminated on a need-to-know basis— and most employees don't need to know much. People will be paid whatever they are worth in the marketplace. And oh, yes: this is a *business*. We need you when we need you, even if it's after hours. If we don't need you, we'll let you know. At any rate, leave your personal life at home. These messages tend to be delivered in starkest form to workers at the bottom of the totem pole. (See, for example, the accounts of low-wage workplaces in Barbara Ehrenreich's best-selling book *Nickel and Dimed*.)[5] But even well-paid white-collar employees often hear much the same song—one reason why the comic strip *Dil-bert* has become so popular among office workers.[6]

Where employees are part of the ownership group, however—when they, too, have claims to the income and wealth generated by their work—the workplace can be organized and run differently, with different expectations of what employee shareholders should do and what responsibilities they should bear. At equity companies such as Gore, the fact of employees' ownership serves as the underpinning for a very different set of messages that the company works hard to transmit. We can't emphasize too much or too often that a different culture doesn't magically appear once employees have company stock, any more than a house erects itself spontaneously once the builder has poured a good concrete foundation. At the risk of oversimplifying, the four central messages that have to be transmitted are something like the following.

Never Forget That You Are Owners as Well as Employees

This may be the most obvious message. All the practices mentioned in the previous chapter—the education, the sharing of business information, the profit sharing and dividends—go far to remind people of their ownership stakes. So does the language that companies use in everyday conversations. Gore's "investment reports" and Robert Mc-Cracken's conversations with manufacturing associates about return on investment are all means to the end of reinforcing ownership. Equity companies typically surround their employees with other ownership messages as well, to the point where they are hard to miss. Business cards say "owner" on them. Marketing materials and Web sites remind the world (and the company's employees) that this company is employee owned. Many companies fly flags and banners that trumpet their employee ownership. They pass out jackets and hats with "ESOP" or "employee owner" stitched into them. In internal communications, where traditional companies tend to use "we" to denote the company and "you" to denote employees, equity companies stick with "we" and "us" for everybody.

King Arthur Flour probably should get the award for most imaginative ownership-related rituals. Employees become eligible for King

Arthur's ESOP after one year of service, and after five years they are 60 percent vested. At that point they receive a clock with the King Arthur logo and their name etched into it—and they are *knighted*. "We have a knighting ceremony!" exclaims Cindy Fountain, the retail manager. "Did you see the sword?" Fountain laughs; the sword is stuck into a "rock" in the company's reception area. She goes on:

> At our annual Twelfth Night party in January, any employee owner who has completed five years of service is celebrated. You receive your title—often created by your fellow employee owners—from president Steve Voigt. He also presents you with a gift, often a hand-blown glass clock engraved with your name and the King Arthur Flour logo. It's a wonderful ceremony.

After seven years King Arthur's employees are fully vested. At that point they receive—a vest.

> And we also have a vesting service, when you're 100 percent vested, the end of your seventh year. You literally get a King Arthur Flour vest! It's very emotional! It's like, you've been here seven years, full-time, you're invested with all of us now. You're greeted by all the employee owners that have already hit this crossroad. When you put that vest on, it's really a great moment. I'm a crier, so I cried. Some people do high fives, happy dances, pump their fists.

At some equity companies, the common (and often derided) "employee of the month" award becomes "employee owner of the month," with as much emphasis on *owner* as on *employee*. "We require certain things" for nomination, explains Steve Graham, the showroom manager at Jackson's Hardware. Going to an "EO of the month" board prominently displayed in the lunchroom, he reads (and paraphrases) the required qualifications:

> Nominees should set an example to other associates in the way they treat and handle our customers. [They should] take pride in ownership; their attitude exemplifies it. They have an understanding of how our ESOP works. The associate is a key player, excellent attendance, they're always there for their

fellow associates, they always do what's best for our store. They're hardworking, very efficient in their time management. They must have one year of employment here at Jackson's. Store managers can't be nominated.

Nor are employees likely to ignore the award:

And what they win! They get use of a gas card for a month. They get a $500 weekend trip or else a shopping spree at Jackson's Hardware, plus dinner at one of the local restaurants for them and their spouse. They'll be entered for Jackson's Hardware ESOP associate of the year. One nominee attends the western-states conference (for employee-owned companies). And our winner for the year gets a trip to Hawaii.

If You Make Your Career Here, You Will Have Opportunities

More than most companies, equity companies seem to promote from within. In fact, some make a point of never looking outside the business until they are sure that no one inside is qualified for whatever position needs filling. "We grow our own leadership here," says John Wegener, firmly. Wegener is plant manager for Scot Forge's Spring Grove, Illinois, facility. "That way, you have a relationship—when you need something done, some kind of interaction between departments, you have a relationship, and people are willing to work together. That feeds the employee-ownership part." Says Gore's McCracken: "To be honest, I can't think of any leader in EPD [electronic products division] that we hired from the outside. We've had some, I guess—but nearly all are from within. They have the credibility with everybody else." As a corollary, companies typically invest considerable amounts not only in training but in rotating promising people through different departments and divisions to get experience. McCracken shakes his head in wonder as he reviews his own thirteen-year career:

In my case, I'd been in the operations side, actually working on connectors, and they asked me if I would work with the manufacturing floor . . . That was the first year I was at Gore. In the other thirteen years, it's been leadership asking me, "Hey, there's a new business we're going to start up . . . would you be able to start this?" Or, "There's a business [where] we just had a product specialist leave, it's sort of in—the marketing, the business leader if you will, go in and figure out, sort of stabilize the operations side." So within EPD I've been with about eight businesses. And all those have been where leadership asked me if I would take on that opportunity.

Equity companies provide other sorts of opportunities as well. Just as bright and ambitious blue-collar workers in days past became shop stewards and union officials, bright and ambitious employee owners find ways to expand their horizons even if they are unable (for whatever reason) to move around and upward in the organization. They volunteer for extra assignments, which are usually plentiful. They join task forces. Many companies with ESOPs have an ESOP committee or council. There are no legal guidelines for what an ESOP committee should do—indeed, there is no legal requirement that a company have one—so committee structures and responsibilities vary widely. Chatsworth Products, a manufacturer headquartered in Westlake Village, California, has committees at each of its five sites. ComSonics, a cable-equipment repair service company in Harrisonburg, Virginia, has an elected committee; would-be members nominate themselves and stage minicampaigns to garner votes. At Gardener's Supply, in Vermont, every employee is assigned to one member of the eleven-person ESOP committee, who then acts as the employee's representative. Gardener's committee members pass out monthly information sheets to their "constituents," help people learn about employee ownership and the company's business performance, and act as a go-between when issues arise in the workplace. "People have felt comfortable coming to us with different issues," says statistical analyst Sherry Ceresa, a committee member, "be it morale issues or be it 'I saw a product in the catalog that I don't feel aligns with our mission and vision, and I'm wondering how it got there.' We don't feel qualified to answer all the questions, so we will reroute them to the people who are. But employees feel more comfortable coming to us."

Committee members also undertake projects that they feel are important to the company's well-being. At Gardener's, committee members Dalton Flint, Tim Lewis, and others were concerned about a split between people who worked in the office (mostly customer-service representatives and corporate staff) and those who worked in the warehouse filling orders. The two facilities are physically separated by the Winooski River, and the physical separation was accompanied by a sense of social separation. "That really disturbed me and was one of my motivations for getting on the ESOP committee: to try and figure out how to alleviate that," says Flint. "It's a definite problem . . . but it was a difficult topic to address. No matter how much you tried to create co-hesiveness, there was still that river between us." One of the commit-tee's ideas: allow people to "shadow" colleagues who worked in the other facility. Lewis explains:

> One of the things that did come out [of the discussion] is job shadowing. Sitting with somebody else who does a completely different job and seeing what their life is like for a day. We've actually started that a little bit between the call center and the workers from the warehouse. Whoever had a really slow time in the summer, whether it was a day or a couple days a week or something . . . They could deal with customers for a day, they could hear what the problems are. I think that's been fairly enlightening.

The tendency of employee owners to build careers with their em-ployers is not lost on these companies' competitors. Take Swinerton, Inc., a San Francisco–based construction company owned by its em-ployees through an ESOP for many years. In a recent conversation with one of the authors (Martin Staubus), the president of another San Francisco construction company—this one conventionally owned—complained of Swinerton, "You can't hire anybody out of that com-pany. When we have a vacancy on our team, we approach people over there about the job, but they're not interested. You can't get them out of there with a crowbar."

You Will Participate in the Running of This Company

Much of the research about employee ownership has found that own-ership makes a difference to a company's performance only when it is coupled with some form of participative or high-performance management. *Participative management* is a phrase that covers a lot of ground, but the idea behind it is simple enough. Employees at participatory companies get a chance—and have the responsibility—to make some of the decisions other companies reserve for management. They get a chance to express their opinions on other decisions, even sizable ones. Thus the teams at Gore set their own schedules and determine much else about how they go about their jobs. The work cells at Stone Construction Equipment track their progress during the day and readjust who's doing what as necessary. Herman Miller teams set economic value added (EVA) goals and then figure out how to meet them. Teamwork of this sort—self-managing teams, cross-functional teams, and so on—is central to participative management, and equity-oriented companies devote considerable time and resources to implementing it. At Whole Foods Market, the big natural-foods chain, every department in every store is a team that, in effect, runs its own little business. Whole Foods teams even make decisions about hiring: new hires are considered provisional for four weeks and must then get a two-thirds vote from team members before they become permanent employees. Because profit-sharing checks are based on team performance, employees don't want "buddies on their teams," reports Charles Fishman of *Fast Company*; they want *workers*—people who are "going to make them some money."[7]

The following chapter will focus on how employees at equity companies participate day in and day out by learning key business disciplines and driving results. But the companies weave participative management into the cultural fabric in other ways as well. We mentioned earlier the classic case of Atlas Container, where the CEO put to the plant employees the choice of which million-dollar machine the company should buy. Whole Foods Market makes a distinction between "consensus" decisions, typically made at the work-team level; "consultative" decisions, made by senior leadership after discussion with those affected; and "command and control decisions," the occasional decision made by a senior leader when time doesn't permit wide consultation.[8] When the company was exploring health insurance alternatives in 2003, it laid out several options and then asked its more than twenty-five thousand employees to vote on them. About 80 percent of employees participated.[9]

Formal votes like those may be rare, but consultation is not. King Arthur Flour has a new warehouse. "Teams of employees who work in the warehouse helped design it," says Steve Voigt, King Arthur's president. "We took the team around to a bunch of other companies, and they saw what they liked and didn't like. We didn't hire a consultant— we just took the consultant money and put it into a contingency fund to fix what we didn't like. And we're still ahead of the game." Scot Forge takes this kind of consultation one step further. As Rick De Rosa, who runs the ring mill and does a number of other jobs in the shop ("call me a jack of all trades"), explains it:

> When they designed the new press console, they asked input from all the press operators. The engineers—instead of saying, this is the way it is, I'm an engineer—they made a drawing, they asked input from all the operators. Then they made a model, and they tried to accommodate everything. They didn't just go and do their engineer thing . . .

In general, adds De Rosa:

> I wouldn't think nothing of it, if we wanted something changed or reengineered a little bit; it's not like I have to go to [plant manager] John Wegener and go through the channels . . . If you wanted some tooling remade or whatever, it's not unheard of to just go to the engineers; they redraw it, shoot it through the system; and the next time we have that job, we got a new tool made to the employees' specs. That's a phenomenal thing, because I know people who work at other companies. What they get is, "This is what we got, like it or leave it." That's not the way it is around here.

At SAIC, one vehicle for involvement is known as the technical environment committee, or TEC. The TEC is formally charged with making sure that the work environment is conducive to high-quality scientific and technical work, but it also serves as a conduit for employee opinions and participation. Several years ago, the company learned from its consultants that health-care costs were likely to rise between 15 and 18 percent one year, and CEO Bob Beyster was concerned that an increase of that magnitude in benefit costs would make its proposals uncompetitive. "So he came to the technical environment committee," remembers nuclear physicist Bill Scott, who was committee chairman at the time, "and he said, 'Rearrange the benefits so that people are happy with their medical and they're happy with everything else, but something's got to be cut.'" Scott continues:

> What we did was reduce our sick leave. We changed our vacation and combined it with sick leave, so if you took extra sick leave, you were actually losing your vacation. But one of the things I was most proud of is that we had these senior management perks at the time. They [senior managers] got extra medical benefits, more than the regular employees. So we took that money and we used it to subsidize the lowest-paid people in the company on their premiums. The senior managers were more than pleased to give up a little perk to feel better about how we were handling the medical.

How many companies would that happen in?

Here, too, we have to give a "most imaginative" award: it goes to Community Provider of Enrichment Services, Inc., which for most of its life was known as Community Psychology & Education Services, but always CPES (pronounced SEE-pus). CPES is a seven-hundred-employee Arizona company that provides services to people with developmental disabilities and mental illness (more on this company in the following chapter). Every year, before the annual meeting, it distributes so-called priority forms, which ask employees to list the issue or issues that they believe CPES should devote attention to during the coming twelve months. Employees each get six votes, which they are free to distribute as they see fit. At first, says cofounder Tom Schramski, if there were seventy-five employees, there would be seventy-five different priorities listed on the forms. And employees were skeptical. "I do remember the first [annual meeting] I came to," recalls Amy Rubinson, a support supervisor, "and quite frankly my attitude was, 'Oh, you know, they're just doing this to make us feel like we have a say, and this is a big joke.'"

That was really how I went in there. And every year we'd write them all down and we'd get our little memo about [them]—and I was like "If these three things aren't taken care of by the end of this year, someone's gonna hear about it." And every time they were! I was really surprised. It changed my attitude. Obviously, you can't deal with everything, but the top things were taken care of. It changed my feeling a lot on that.

As they learned that the company took the votes seriously, employees grew more sophisticated about what they asked for. Says regional director Bob Bennetti:

When we did the priority forms six, seven years ago, it was all "Let's put a Jacuzzi in the office," stuff we were never going to do. But now we've done a good job of teaching people that we're going to pay attention to what you want. And I think the staff has gotten together and figured out "Let's not waste our vote. These are the big things." Health insurance is big. Increased direct-care wage, the starting wage, is big. It's almost like a conspiracy! . . . No more goofing around about an employee lunchroom, a new microwave. We don't need stuff like that. But in the old days, we used to get that stuff all the time.

In recent years, says Schramski, health insurance premiums have been at the top of the list by far—and the company has responded to employee concerns by expanding its coverage. "Sure, there was a financial burden associated with it," explains Schramski. "But I thought it was good, first of all because everybody should have health-care coverage. But the other thing was, it solidified the relationship with those folks. If we can keep them around longer, it makes all the difference in the world: it adds to quality, adds to the relationship [with clients], reduces our liability, reduces the cost of training and turnover."

We Are All in This Together

When he was CEO of Southwest Airlines, Herb Kelleher famously made a practice of spending the occasional day on the front lines. He slung bags on the ramp. He worked the customer-service desk. Following

Kelleher's lead, Southwest has instituted a variety of programs aimed at giving people a sense of one another's jobs. Under the so-called cutting edge program, for instance, pilots spend a day working as ramp agents to "learn about what goes on around the plane and in its belly while it's at the gate."[10] Such practices send a powerful message to employees, to the effect that everybody's work is valued, and nobody's above helping out somebody else. Many of the equity companies we visited promote the same kind of ethos, even with some of the same practices. At Gardener's Supply, for instance, everybody pitches in during peak season to help answer the phones and pack boxes; among the helpers are CEO Will Raap, president Jim Feinson, and chief operating officer Cindy Turcot. It doesn't go unnoticed. Says Sherry Ceresa, the statistical analyst:

> At holiday time primarily if we have a lot of packages to pack in our warehouse, we'll go over after work hours, and we'll pack boxes. And Will Raap will be right next to you. Jim Feinson will be up on the phones. There's a sheet that goes around, and nine times out of ten he'll leave himself till last. He'll take the crappy hours that are left over. Or if there's an extra spot, he'll take it! And you'll be standing next to Cindy opening mail. That, to me, shows they thoroughly believe that it's everybody's company. They're not sitting in their offices.

Out of curiosity, we made a point of asking frontline employees in the companies we visited how sharp their own job boundaries were. For example, were people permitted to say, "That's not my job," when asked to do something out of the ordinary? Most of our respondents looked at us sort of incredulously. Thus Scot Forge's Leo Szlembarski:

> Nope. You don't hear that here. I worked here so many years and you don't hear that. I've never heard that. I've heard it other places, not here.

But what if someone's regular job is interrupted, and he or she has nothing to do? Rick De Rosa shakes his head:

> There aren't a lot of folks standing around. It's kind of the Scot Forge way. There's always work to be done. Even if we're not making production. You can straighten up; there's always

straightening up to be done. We work with steel, so scale falls off it. Twice a week we have to shovel out the pit in the ring mill. So if there's no rings to roll one day, you've got the opportunity to spend a couple hours in the pit.

Jackson's Hardware president and general manager Bill Loskutoff describes the environment he wants to see in the store and how he views his own role:

There's no "not my job." The ones that say that don't last very long . . . Every once in a while our bathroom gets plugged up. And if I'm the one that somebody tells, I'll clean it. I will do those jobs. I will not ask an associate to do something I wouldn't do. And they know that. Nor will they say, "That's not my job." If there's a physical problem, somebody's coming back from a work injury, [that's different]. For a long time we didn't have a janitorial person . . . we rotated it through everybody in the store. The front counter took care of one bathroom, the back counter took care of another bathroom, the warehouse took care of another, and they rotated it through everybody. Managers, supervisors, and there was no problem, no "It's not my job." It's your *company*. It's not your job, but it's your company.

Jackson's, interestingly, is in an industry where "spiffs" are common: salespeople get little rewards—maybe $5 or a T-shirt—from product manufacturers for selling the manufacturer's product. Jackson's allows no individual to accept a spiff. Says Loskutoff:

What we do here at the store is that all those spiffs . . . go into a kitty, and they're shared amongst all the associates. Because to sell that tool, somebody has to check it in. Somebody has to stock it. Somebody has to sell it. Somebody has to take care of the paperwork—if it's an A/R account or cash account, there are different people involved in that whole transaction . . .

So everybody understands that this is how it operates . . . We've had vendors bring in a dozen jackets or T-shirts that they want to give to specific people. The rule is, we have sixty-seven associates. If you want to make sure that some specific associate gets that jacket, you need to bring sixty-seven, because everybody's going to get the jacket. Otherwise, all the stuff goes up into my office. And when I get to the point where I can't take the clutter any more, we put together sixty-seven grab bags, and they're brought down here to the meeting room, and everybody has a chance at a grab bag. You just take. Who knows what's in there? Somebody might get a mug. There's usually jackets and hats and T-shirts and various things. But it's shared.

In other words, we're all in this together.

Social events reinforce that message. Many companies know this—that's why they have holiday parties and picnics—but most do a lousy job at it. Southwest Airlines, by contrast, is famous (some would say infamous) for the popular celebrations and parties it sponsors, usually complete with costumes. (Kelleher liked to show up on a Harley-Davidson motorcycle, dressed in his own unique version of motorcycle-gang apparel.) Most of the other equity companies go equally far, albeit in their own style. "Every year, we close the company down, usually in June, this year in September, and we have a meal, and we have a company meeting," says Winston Rost of Green Mountain Coffee Roasters. "And then there are games—a rock-climbing wall, tug-of-war, whatever." Jennifer Herman, who handles benefits administration at Scot Forge, describes that company's active social life:

I think another thing, too, that makes us feel like owners and a family is that we have a lot of social events. [Most companies] might have a couple of them, but, my goodness, this year I think we ended up with nine! Eight or nine, throughout the year. Our company picnic in July, where we had nine hundred people attending, that's a family event. We had a canoe trip, a golf outing, and clay shooting, followed by a picnic. The Christmas party—we have over five hundred people that attend that—it becomes a weekend! We did a bowling thing, but we kind of gave that up. We have our annual service awards, where we acknowledge everybody for every five years of service, and we also have Peter I. Georgeson winners. Peter I. Georgeson is chairman of the board, the original founder. It's kind of a peer award. A lot of people in production, office, supervisory, top management, just who you feel made the biggest contribution. You're voted on by your peers. So there's about six winners for that. And then we recognize everybody in October; there's usually one hundred fifty people that attend that every year.

Fun times sort of permeate these businesses, setting them apart from companies that offer their employees little more than a job and a paycheck. Jackson's Hardware sends a few employees—chosen by lot—to Hawaii each year. A few years ago it sent *every* associate. At Gardener's Supply, on the day we visited, one of the employees had organized a spontaneous boccie tournament, and COO Cindy Turcot had to postpone the interview so she could take part. Turcot puts the frivolity in a business context:

> To me, it comes down to, Do you like where you work? There are cynics about the ESOP . . . but if we're here for the culture, which many of us are, we like working here, we like to be empowered, we like to be asked our opinions, and we're not leaving . . . [And] so is it worth it that I don't have 20 percent or 30 percent turnover? Absolutely! It costs a lot of money to have turnover.
>
> I don't know, for me it's worth it. I want to be here. I want to play in boccie tournaments because someone has the guts to just send out an e-mail from the graphic design department and say, "Hey, want to have a boccie tournament?" And you get fifty, sixty people that signed up! And who is he? He's a graphic designer . . . It's not like he had my job. And it created its own life.

The acid test of any we're-all-in-this-together culture, of course, is what happens in a serious business downturn. Most businesses reorganize, cut the budget, offer buyout packages, or simply lay people off. Equity companies—which make such a point of ownership and equal involvement in the business—can't easily rely on layoffs. Hypertherm, the New Hampshire–based manufacturer of plasma cutting machines, in fact adheres to a strict no-layoff policy. "We will never turn to a layoff situation unless we're all going down together," says human resources director Brenda Blair. To be sure, many companies have proclaimed such a policy only to reverse it in exceptionally hard times (IBM and Kodak both come to mind). Hypertherm attempts to manage its growth through outsourcing and overtime, hiring people only when absolutely necessary—and so far has never had a layoff.

Not many equity companies go that far. What they do instead is three things: keep everybody informed about their business situation, get employees involved in figuring out new ways to increase sales or cut costs, and take interim belt-tightening measures short of a layoff. Stone Construction Equipment implemented a 5 percent pay cut when business was slow. Employees at Travel and Transport took voluntary time off. To be sure, there are times when layoffs can't be avoided, and the experience at equity companies is particularly painful. Thus King Arthur Flour, for example, let twenty-one people go in spring 2003. ("I don't know if I'm over it yet," said Cindy Fountain, the retail store manager, some six months later.) Then again, neither did the layoffs come out of the blue, as they do at so many companies. People knew that times were bad, and several employees told us they respected the CEO for making what they felt must have been a tough decision.

The tension, of course, reflects a fundamental difference about equity companies, namely that labor isn't simply a factor of production. Critics have charged that employee-owned companies would protect employment at all costs, and there may be cases where that is true. But there are incentives in the other direction as well. The fewer people on the payroll, the fewer people there are to divide up ownership of the business—and besides, no one wants to see a fellow owner let go. So equity companies tend to run lean. They tend to cut every other possible cost before they cut employment. If there is a price to be paid, it is that they cannot staff up and cut back as quickly or as easily as conventional companies.

IS IT WORTH IT?

That kind of labor-force inflexibility isn't the only potential drawback of creating an ownership culture. Decisions that involve people usually require more time. Meetings are frequent and can be a burden. At

ESOP-owned Kindermusik International, a small company based in Greensboro, North Carolina, every employee attends a fifteen-minute meeting every day; other, longer meetings are held at a variety of levels throughout the year. To keep people on their toes, people are literally on their feet—they stand throughout the meeting. Ask Gore associates about the need for meetings, and they are likely to smile and roll their eyes. "It can be a problem," acknowledged Jim Buckley. "You'll hear that comment within Gore. 'Ohhh, another meeting!'" What it boils down to is that such a culture is an investment that requires considerable time and effort to maintain. It isn't just the meetings, it's the fact that somebody needs to be paying attention. Gore, for instance, mounted a companywide reexamination of the entire culture a few years ago. The purpose was partly to see what changes might need to be made, but also to reacquaint associates with the ideas behind the culture and to reinvolve them in maintaining it. The series of off-site meetings, along with all the time spent on preparation and follow-up, must have cost the company hundreds of thousands of dollars.

An equity culture raises two other sorts of issues as well. One is how widely applicable it is—whether a Gore-type culture, for instance, could be transferred to a company with a different history or business model. Gore's focus on innovation is central to its business success. The company attracts a certain kind of person, namely those who thrive in an intense but often unstructured environment. A lot of people would be more comfortable in a more traditional workplace, where they knew who their boss was and what they were expected to do. Similarly, not every retail or manufacturing employee would be comfortable with Jackson's Hardware's or Stone Construction Equipment's firm expectation that you will go wherever you are needed.

A second issue is that the benefits of an equity culture can be hard to quantify. You can't run a controlled experiment in business, so you have to rely on companies' perceptions as to whether it is all worth it. Gore and the others do swear by their cultures. Senior executives believe that the way their employees or associates think and act is a critical ingredient of their business success. They can point to some measurable effects, such as low turnover and high employee satisfaction. Whether the benefits are worth the costs is, however, at least partly a leap of faith. The research referred to in the previous chapter suggests that it is, but a skeptic might ask whether a particular company such as Gore or Jackson's needs to go as far as it does to get its business results.

On the other hand, we're not sure that anyone needs to quantify the effect of individual employees going the extra mile, figuring out how to save money or how to take care of customers better, without prompting from management or anybody else, which is essentially what all these cultural messages encourage. A customer-service rep at Phelps County Bank learned elementary Farsi and Chinese—really—the better to serve the many international students studying at the local branch of the University of Missouri. A long-term worker at McKay Nursery, who had started as a seasonal employee, came up with an idea for reducing the labor involved in covering the company's hoophouses every winter, saving perhaps $10,000 annually. Then there's Karen Adolphson, an accountant at Jackson's Hardware. In 2003, when her children were five and three, she had an idea: why didn't the store sell a few toys at Christmastime? It would be a way of attracting more customers and of keeping the kids happy while their parents shopped. She talked it over with a few coworkers and brought it up at the company's so-called carrot club, a group devoted to business-improvement ideas. Getting a positive response, she did some research and found a couple of dozen items that she thought might be hard to find in an ordinary toy store—balsa wood airplanes, "rocket" cars propelled by baking soda and vinegar, 1950s-style metal dump trucks, and the like. Acting as buyer, she placed the orders. When the goods arrived, she worked in the warehouse, making sure they got properly checked in and stocked. Jackson's did a fast business in toys that season. And Adolphson, like so many of the employees or associates of equity companies, got some hands-on experience in thinking and acting like a business owner. In the cultural environment created by founder H. C. Jackson and carried on by Bill Loskutoff and the other leaders at Jackson's Hardware, Adolphson's initiative seemed somehow perfectly normal.

Running the Business

By themselves, equity ownership and an ownership-oriented culture go far toward transforming the workplace. They help—and remind—employees to see their role differently. But historically, these changes have suffered from a serious drawback: companies find it hard to sustain the enthusiasm and commitment they engender. Senior leaders may be supportive, since it is usually they who introduced the changes. But they often feel more pressing priorities than making sure the changes last. Meanwhile, middle managers must learn new skills for which they may not be well suited, such as helping employees learn to make their own decisions. It can be hard for these managers to deal with the ambiguity involved—"OK, what *exactly* am I supposed to do now?"—and some are likely to feel threatened by the potential loss of their authority. Frontline employees themselves are often skeptical. Any change at all these days is automatically written off as the "flavor of the month," at least for a while. But even if employees get past their initial doubts, not all will buy in. They, too, are being asked to learn more, to take on more responsibility, and to work with other people in a more cooperative fashion. Human relations theorists sometimes assume that everybody wants to work in this manner. Not everybody does.

Some companies get past these roadblocks through persistence alone. Typically, they rely on a leader—usually a chief executive—who is passionately committed to the new way of doing things and who hammers relentlessly on ownership, on communication, on participation, on celebrations, and on all the other cultural artifacts that contribute to the equity model. These leaders—Bob Beyster of SAIC is one, Jack Stack of SRC is another—put ownership at the top of their priority list. They experiment with different forms and with different ways of reinforcing the message. They borrow good ideas from other companies. They learn from what doesn't work as well as what does. They follow the advice of Tom Peters—if it ain't broke, fix it anyway— which is to say that they are constantly experimenting with new variations on the ownership theme. These companies typically go about their business like any other company, but they leave no doubt in anyone's mind about the fact that employees are also owners.

In recent years a relative handful of companies, including some that we studied, have gone one step further. They rely on all the practices just mentioned, and they are just as dependent as any company on commitment from top management. But they have also learned how to incorporate the expectation that employees will think and act like owners *into the way they operate the company*. They teach employees the fundamental disciplines that drive the business, and then build employee involvement into everyday performance management. *Participation* in these companies means more than serving on a committee or helping to decide your work group's schedule. It means taking joint responsibility with your co-workers for your part of the business—and for moving whatever needle gauges your unit's performance. At these companies, a change in senior leadership won't necessarily mean the end of the ownership culture.

Again, this is an easier notion to grasp when you can see it in practice. Our exemplar this time around is Community Provider of Enrichment Services (formerly Community Psychology & Education Services, but then and now CPES), in Arizona. We'll describe CPES's approach and then dissect this third part of our model to see how it works in a variety of contexts.

THE NEW ECONOMY'S OTHER SIDE

CPES represents what might be called the other side of America's new economy—not the glamorous, high-tech arena but the part in which (mostly) low-wage workers provide hands-on services to people who need them. Thus the fastest-growing markets these days include not just biotech and the Internet but mundane businesses such as home health care and personal services. CPES's niche, so far, has been to provide care for people with severe developmental disabilities and mental illness—people who find it difficult to get and keep a job, to live independently, or in some cases even to feed and care for themselves. It's a task that in the past would have been done exclusively by state agencies or by nonprofits, and in some states still is. But governments have been contracting out more of the service-providing chores they once did themselves, and more for-profit companies such as CPES are entering these markets. As the population ages, some of these providers are likely to expand into related but potentially much larger markets, such as the business of taking care of the elderly in their own homes. "There's a big demand for those services," says Tom Schramski, cofounder of CPES and until recently its CEO. "It's going to go through the roof."[1]

Schramski, born in 1951, grew up in Mankato, Minnesota. As a child, he helped out at the two independent gas stations his father ran. But in 1973—after "too many twenty-below station openings in the early morning"—he moved to Arizona, completed his BA at Prescott College, and went on to earn a PhD in psychology from the University of Arizona. Entrepreneurship came upon him sort of by accident. In February 1980, the State of Arizona settled a lawsuit brought by advocacy groups for people with developmental disabilities. The state agreed to phase out the few large facilities in which it cared for these people. Instead, it would seek out organizations that could provide less restrictive community-based care. Schramski and a partner, David Harvey, decided to enter the business, and set up a company they called Counseling & Consulting Services. The market was wide open—"There were only a couple of provider organizations like ours" at the time, says Schramski—and the company grew. Harvey left in 1984 to pursue a consulting practice, taking the name with him. But Schramski stayed on to run the newly christened Community Psychology & Education Services.

The business did well. It grew steadily, if slowly, and it earned modest profits. But there were tensions, both external and internal. On the outside, the State of Arizona, which issued CPES's contracts, seemed ambivalent about for-profit companies. "In 1992 the state put provider organizations under a microscope," Schramski remembers.

> I was in the paper. Everybody was in the paper. They said things like, "CPES spent $27.37 on flowers!" Maybe we gave flowers to somebody's family after somebody died . . . All this stuff. Even though our rates were the same as every other organization's. They were trying to drive a wedge between for-profit and not-for-profit.

Advocacy groups and clients' families could sometimes be distrustful as well. Are you going to make money off taking care of our daughter? Is it right that you should *profit* from providing services to these needy people? Internally, Schramski was learning the difficulties of running a service business in which reimbursement rates—hence the company's revenue—were determined by a penurious government agency. The company could pay its frontline workers only a dollar an hour more than the minimum wage. The work was difficult and demanding, both physically and emotionally. Clients often needed help with the most basic of functions. Some could be obstreperous, sullen, or otherwise "cognitively challenged." So employee turnover was high. Schramski and his managers were perpetually scrambling to make sure that client care didn't suffer from the revolving door on the front lines.

At some point in the early 1990s, not long after the state's investigation, Schramski had an epiphany. Or rather a pair of epiphanies. He read an article about employee ownership and invited one of us (Corey Rosen) to make a presentation on the subject to the company. He read *The Great Game of Business*, in which SRC's Jack Stack (with Bo Burlingham) explains the system of open-book management he had developed at his company. Employee ownership, Schramski came to realize, would cut right through the for-profit/not-for-profit dichotomy. CPES could continue to operate as a for-profit enterprise, but it would be benefiting the people who actually did the work—hard for either the state or clients' families to object to. Moreover, sharing the wealth, opening the books, and getting employees involved in the business in the manner described by Stack might cut down on turnover and make for a more stable, more productive organization. Selling stock to an

ESOP, not incidentally, would provide Schramski with liquidity and an exit strategy, should he ever decide to move on to something else.

In 1995 Schramski signed the papers to set up an ESOP, selling 50.1 percent of his stock to the plan. Later he sold it the rest, making CPES a company wholly owned by its employees. That was the simple part, as it turned out. The hard part was helping people on the staff learn to think and act like owners. Employees at CPES were even more uncertain about ownership than employees in more conventional industries. They were particularly leery of anything that smelled of finance. "A lot of us come from a social-work kind of background," says Bob Bennetti, CPES's regional director for southern Arizona, "and talking about the bottom line, revenue, margins, and that stuff is—not that it's hard, but it's almost distasteful, because what people think is that it compromises your decisions in terms of the quality of care. And so I think that was the resistance initially." Some people left. Others dragged their heels. As at a lot of companies, enthusiasm for the new ideas waxed and waned depending on how hard Schramski and other leaders pushed them. "In the first couple of years, we got people interested in it," Schramski recalled in late 2003. "Then we had a trough for a couple of years in there, where we didn't stay at it. And then the last couple or three years, we brought it back."

Today, CPES could be a poster child for employee ownership in this kind of service business. It has continued to grow steadily: its payroll now numbers more than seven hundred, while its revenues total roughly $22 million. It has offices in both Tucson—company headquarters—and Phoenix, and it operates close to one hundred group homes and other facilities. Its profits are still modest—caring for this clientele is not exactly a high-margin endeavor—but they are steady, and its stock value has increased. Turnover dropped from 100 percent per year to (at last report) below 60 percent, a huge cost savings and an obvious benefit to CPES's clientele. A few senior employees already have six-figure balances in their ESOP accounts. When families interview CPES as part of the process of choosing a provider, company representatives let them know that CPES is owned by its employees, and are glad to share the company's financials with them. "The reaction to the employee ownership has been very, very positive" from families, says Schramski.

But what's most remarkable about the company is its system of management, which is modeled on the approach taken by Stack at SRC. To get a feel for it, sit in on one of the company's regional meetings, known as huddles.

THE HUDDLE

This particular huddle—October 23, 2003—takes place in a big meeting room at the Rodeway Inn, just off the interstate in Tucson. Maybe sixty people are gathered around the tables, which are set up party-style with paper tablecloths. Most are laughing and joking noisily, which to a visitor seems incongruous because the meeting's ostensible purpose is to review the southern Arizona region's financial performance for the previous quarter. Equally incongruous, though in keeping with the jovial mood, are the noisemakers, confetti, and cans of Silly String that cover the tables. The group includes Schramski, then still the CEO; Bennetti, the regional director; the other managers and supervisors for the southern Arizona region; a couple of dozen front-line employees, and at least one *consumer*, which is the word CPES folks use to refer to the people they serve.

It soon becomes plain that this is no ordinary review meeting. The financials projected on a screen up front are simplified: they include eight lines of dollar figures, from revenue to net operating margin, and a couple of ratios, such as salaries as a percent of revenue. They are broken down by team. (A team is responsible for several care facilities.) Each team's leader walks the whole group through its numbers. The energy level is higher than most companies would see at a meeting to announce bonuses. Good results bring whoops, hollers, rounds of applause. Not-so-good numbers earn the speaker catcalls and shots of Silly String. Every number is compared with the company's plan. Here, for example, is Linki Peddy, associate director for the Tucson area:

> OK, these are our numbers for our day service sites here in the Tucson area. We actually did better than we had anticipated, although we're still striving to do better. We thought that we would have an income of $137,000; we actually brought in

$138,000, even more than that, which put us to the good by
$1,200. Year to date, we're tracking about $9,700 over what we
anticipated . . .

   For salaries we anticipated that we would be spending
about $98,000; we actually only spent $88,000 . . . Year to date
we're tracking about $25,000 under what we had anticipated
[for salaries]. Salaries as a percent of revenue, we are tracking
well below what we had anticipated, which was 71 percent, and
we're at 64 percent. [Applause, shrieks.] Buildings and grounds
maintenance and repair, we're doing well; we're under what we
had anticipated year to date. In fact, the only thing we're running over on is building and grounds maintenance for September. [Noise; someone in the front row shoots Silly String.]

   Program support costs [PSC], we're doing better than anticipated: $2,600 last month, year to date we're tracking almost
$8,000 under what we had anticipated. PSC as a percent of rev-
enue, also tracking below what we had anticipated. Net operating
income, we anticipated $15,000 for the month; we actually made
just under $27,000, and $37,000 for year to date. So the bottom
line is, we anticipated 11.2 percent [and] we actually did 19.5 before administrative expenses; year to date we're tracking about 20
percent. So overall we are doing much better than anticipated,
and it's getting better and better. [Whoops, cheers, etc.]

   We quote this at length just to underscore a couple of points. Peddy
is not a member of CPES's financial staff. Her audience includes most of
the managers and supervisors in the region, plus plenty of line employees—people with little or no formal training in finance. Yet all seem to
be following the simplified financials that are projected on the screen,
and several will themselves take a turn leading the group through the
numbers that they are responsible for. Near the end, regional director
Bennetti will take people through the region's consolidated financials,
again at the same level of detail: performance for the quarter, compared
with plan; performance year to date, compared with plan.

   After the financials come numbers related to the quality of CPES's
services. Licensing violations, if any. (In this business there are always

one or two.) Unusual-incident reports, required by the state for incidents such as a client hitting somebody. Staff turnover. Workers' compensation. But then after these numbers comes something quite different: stories of individual consumers and how they are progressing. Harold S. had to leave the family that was supporting him, but is now safely ensconced in a small CPES group home. David P. had been "chased out of his community" because of a couple of incidents; he, too, is now safely in a CPES home. A young woman, a CPES consumer, is brought to a high school football game, where she meets up with her friends; the CPES staff member is able to leave and come back later to pick her up, a sign of her growing ability to function independently. Each story brings applause, laced with hollers of approval. The accounts are heartwarming and poignant, and obviously serve to remind the group of why they're in this business at all.

Finally come a dozen or so awards for employees who have gone beyond the call of duty over the past quarter. Again, different people take turns announcing the awards—but each one calls out, "Drum roll, please," before the announcement, and the assembled men and women beat energetically on the tables with their hands. Marcie Brown, a supervisor at the site known as Coral, gets an award for coming in at midnight one night when the pipes broke, and again when the roof collapsed after a torrential downpour. The "job developers" on Peddy's team—people who help find gainful employment for consumers who are able to work—get an award. So do the three people on the community resource committee—Shannon, Shana, and Jeff—for everything they have done on their own time at the company's community resource center. A picture of a dance at the center goes up on the screen. All told, more than a dozen awards are handed out.

The whole thing lasts a little over an hour. People then help themselves to pizza and soft drinks, provided by the company.

BUSINESS DISCIPLINE

We'll analyze this huddle in more depth throughout the rest of this chapter and compare it with what other companies do. First, we need to step back and establish a context for understanding what's going on.

As we observed in chapter 2, standout companies succeed over time usually because they have learned and pursued a particular set of disciplines to a point that competitors find difficult to match. No news here: numberless management writers have described Wal-Mart's unparalleled information systems, Procter & Gamble's time-honored marketing abilities, Dell Computer Corporation's world-class direct-sales expertise and just-in-time manufacturing system. What distinguishes equity companies is that they have also developed a different kind of discipline, namely the discipline of getting people to work together efficiently and effectively. They engage every employee in learning and practicing whatever other disciplines determine the company's success, and thus in moving the needle of business performance in the right direction. They get employees thinking and acting not just like "owners" in the abstract but like *partners in the enterprise*—like businesspeople.

Southwest Airlines is a good example. The company has been phenomenally successful in a notoriously tough business, recording an unbroken string of profitable years while the rest of the industry seesaws from losses to profits and back again. (Recently, Southwest's market capitalization has been larger than that of all the other airlines combined.) It has fought off direct challenges from much larger airlines—United, for example—that tried to emulate its no-frills business model. Southwest's central discipline, of course, is its ability to keep costs, hence fares, low. It pursues that discipline in any number of ways. It avoids congested airports. It buys only one kind of airplane, thereby minimizing training and maintenance costs. It refuses to assign seats and doesn't serve meals. One key element of low-cost operation is its ability to "turn" airplanes—to get them back in the air, thus earning money—faster than other airlines. This, as Southwest people are quick to remind you, is not a matter of "tricks," it's a matter of carefully developed choreography on the part of every participant and a willingness on the part of employees to do whatever is necessary to accomplish the goal. Writers Kevin and Jackie Freiberg observed a turn one afternoon at Los Angeles International airport and chronicled every move. Their account (slightly abridged):

2:45 P.M. Like a finely honed pit crew waiting for that Indy car to arrive, Rudy Guidi, Calvin Williams, Kirkland Howling, and Ricardo Pérez prepare to spring into action. Rudy and Calvin go over the bin sheet, which tells the team how much baggage, freight, and mail is on the aircraft, while the rest of the team makes sure the equipment is in position to turn the plane. The ground crew is joined by First Officer Ken Brown, who is there to do a preflight check on the aircraft.

2:46 P.M. The aircraft is in sight, and Ricardo jumps up on the back of the tug to guide the plane into the jetway. Rudy and Calvin each start up a belt loader and begin to move toward the plane as it approaches the gate.

2:47 P.M. The aircraft comes to a complete stop at the gate. The jetway is already moving toward the door of the aircraft. The baggage bins of the Boeing 737 fly open. A fueler pulls up to the aircraft while crew members off-load bags.

2:48 P.M. Ken pauses for a moment from his preflight check to help Kirkland connect the pushback to the nose gear of the airplane. Provisioning crew members race through the rear door of the aircraft to stock ice, drinks, and snacks and to empty trash. Passengers begin to deplane . . .

2:50 P.M. First officer completes his preflight check. Flight attendants move through the cabin of the aircraft to reposition seat belts and pick up trash.

2:51 P.M. All bags are off-loaded. Ramp agents begin loading bags for new passengers. Provisioning is complete . . . Operations agent makes initial announcement calling for preboarders . . . Fueler is pulling the hose out of the wing of the aircraft.

2:52 P.M. Operations agent begins boarding customers in groups of thirty. Bags are loaded and fueling is complete. Most of the ground crew move to another gate to prepare for the arrival of the next aircraft.

3:00 P.M. Passenger boarding is complete; operations agent gives weight and balance sheet to pilot. Pilots trim the aircraft according to the load. Ramp agent connects the communication gear to talk to the pilots in the cockpit from the tarmac.

3:01 P.M. The jetway pulls back and the door of the aircraft closes. Pushback maneuvers the plane onto the tarmac and turns

the plane toward the runway. Ramp agent unhooks the pushback from the aircraft and the plane taxies toward the runway.

During this sixteen-minute period, the Freibergs point out, the various groups of employees deplaned 137 passengers and boarded another 137; accomplished a complete change of flight crew; unloaded
and reloaded bags, mail, and freight; pumped four thousand five hundred pounds of jet fuel into the airplane; and of course got the plane
turned around and ready for takeoff. "People come out of nowhere
and the entire area around the plane is abuzz. Then, in a matter of
minutes, their jobs complete, the swarm of people disappears and the
plane pulls away."[2] What makes it all work is that employees aren't just
dancers in these elaborately scripted steps, they are choreographers as
well. They can add, delete, or change steps—whatever will help them
succeed at the task.

This kind of rigorous discipline is exactly what we saw at Stone
Construction Equipment. At Stone, the dance is slower, since the point
isn't to turn a plane in fifteen minutes but to produce a certain number
of machines in an eight-hour shift. Still, it's equally well scripted and
equally participatory. Employees move from one job to another in
keeping with the day's production schedule. They discuss the schedule
and commit to producing so many parts in each shift. They assess their
performance against scoreboards as the day progresses so that they
can make adjustments as necessary. All the time, they watch the labor
variance numbers to make sure that the work they are doing is cost-
effective. This discipline is what enables Stone to produce its machines
to an individual customer's order and get them out the door quickly—
so quickly, in fact, that the company regards the exact time it takes to
build any one item as a trade secret. In both cases, Southwest's and
Stone's, what *has* to be done is no mystery. But both companies have an
ability to *get* it done by willing employees, people who pitch in and do
whatever is necessary because of their employee ownership and the
culture they have created around that ownership. To these employees,
the goals of quick turnaround or building so many machines aren't just
dicta handed down by management. They're an intrinsic part of what
makes the business successful. The employees understand their part of
the disciplines that allow their company to make money.

Jack Stack, of SRC, merely extended this notion to its logical conclusion. His central insight was that the ultimate discipline in any business is to make the financial results turn out right—and that *employees can get directly involved in that process*. They can learn to understand the key financial numbers, whether of the whole company or of their own business unit or department. They can monitor and track those numbers. They can use the financial results to guide what they do every day on the job. That idea is at the heart of what Stack calls the "great game of business," and what has come to be known generically as open-book management. It is open-book because nothing is hidden; people see key financial metrics and learn to understand them. But it is open-book *management* because the whole point is for employees to help run the business by moving the numbers in the right direction.

KEY ELEMENTS

That's essentially what's going on at CPES. Scrutinize each element of the approach and you will see how.

Establishing Metrics

Business is a game of numbers, so it is said, and learning to be a partner in the business means learning which numbers matter and what each one means. Typically, equity companies focus on one or a few *critical numbers*—the numbers that will mean the difference between success and failure—and then help frontline managers and employees understand them. For the ramp and ground-operations employees at Southwest, turnaround time is one such number. For the shop-floor workers at Stone, it's labor variance. For those at Nypro, it's profit per machine and the other numbers that are on the daily report described by CEO Brian Jones (chapter 5). SAIC, which lives and dies with proposals and contracts, has traditionally watched three key operational variables (number of proposals submitted, number of contracts awarded, and time utilization of professional personnel) and three financial ones (revenues, revenue growth, and profits). "We have a discipline all the way from the division level up" monitoring those figures, says executive vice president Joe Walkush. "We try to keep it simple, just the important numbers." At one point not long ago, the company realized that its receivables were stretching out too long, so it added one last metric—imputed interest on receivables—to its "watch" list.

CPES looks at those key quality indicators, such as license violations, and a simplified income statement that includes the following line items and ratios:

Revenue

Total salaries/ERE (employment-related expenses)

Salaries overtime

Salaries as a percent of revenue

Vehicle maintenance and repair

Buildings/grounds maintenance and repair

Program support cost (PSC)

PSC as a percent of revenue

Net operating income (dollars)

Net operating margin (percent)

Note two things about this selection. One, it focuses on the numbers that matter. There is a *line of sight* between hitting the targets on these numbers and succeeding as a company. In a human services business, these line items, particularly salaries and other personnel expenses, are the key costs, and the difference between making money and not making money lies in controlling those costs. CPES employees know that overtime in particular can be a killer. "People are more willing to help each other out" because they know the numbers, says Steve Ross, a service coordinator. "If somebody's short staffed and somebody else has extra staff, they'll help out instead of putting someone in for OT." Program support cost—which Bob Bennetti likes to call an "index of bureaucracy"—is another. So long as the company can control its personnel costs and keep PSC where it belongs, it has a good chance of winding up in the black.

Two, the list focuses on items that employees and supervisors can control or influence without harming quality. Food expenses aren't on it, because the company doesn't want its staff trying to cut corners with consumers' diets. But maintenance and repair of facilities and vehicles are numbers that can be watched closely, and are. "It has certainly made a difference in terms of people's attention—things that you wouldn't pay attention to ordinarily," says Bennetti. "Vehicle maintenance is an example." At a conventional company, a vehicle in the shop for repairs is a good excuse to rent a nice car—"and what do I care what I'm paying for it, I'll keep it an extra two, three days. But if I'm seeing the budget every month, I'm more likely to go, 'I'm going to go bug the mechanic; I got to get that vehicle today.'"

Understanding and Communicating the Numbers

To reach the point where CPES and other open-book companies are today, most companies find that they have to do a good deal of focused financial-literacy training, of the sort discussed in chapter 5. CPES itself began with a modest brochure titled "The Wild and Wacky World of Financial Literacy." But classes and training programs rarely have any lasting effect unless people get a chance to deepen their knowledge and put it to work—to get some on-the-job training. One of the main businesses of Jack Stack's company, SRC, is remanufacturing heavy-duty engines for use in trucks and farm machinery. Workers take old, worn-out engines, salvage what they can use, throw out what they can't, and rebuild the engine using a combination of original parts and replacement parts. In other words, they have to make hundreds of decisions a day about whether it is worth trying to salvage a particular part, or whether it makes more sense to chuck it and put in a replacement. Stack helped them learn the economics of these decisions: to compare the price of a replacement part with the labor time (including overhead) involved in salvaging one.

At CPES, frontline supervisors help construct the budgets for their individual services. "We put the budget together from the ground up," says Schramski. "So that could be a supervisor, GED level, that's managing a $150,000 program.[3] And they know their budget backwards and forwards. They're building in expectations about certain costs—for example, next year they may know their lease is going to go up by $200 a month. They fill all that stuff in." For Amy Rubinson, who describes herself as "not a big number cruncher," the process was an eye-opener:

"Having to deal with budgets as a supervisor . . . now that everything is open, we can really see the company as a whole and see where the impact is. It has given us a better picture of [what's going on]. Because you have to fit your needs for your consumers, the ones that you are directly responsible for 24/7, into that whole picture."

Another way of learning something, of course, is to teach it—and CPES, like most such companies, makes a point of asking many different people to walk their peers through a review of key results. That's why all the team leaders took a turn at the front of the room, risking the Silly String and catcalls, instead of having a more professional presentation from someone on the finance staff.

Managing the Numbers

The financials, of course, reflect the results of the past quarter or year. Running the business purely on the basis of the financials has been compared to driving by looking in the rearview mirror. So equity companies that use some form of open-book management find ways to track and monitor business performance as it's happening. They create scoreboards—physical or virtual—to track key operational numbers, such as the week's shipments or hours billed for professional personnel. They review financial results as frequently as possible. Cisco Systems is able to close its books on a daily basis. SRC produces an income statement every two weeks. Foldcraft, an employee-owned Minnesota-based manufacturer of restaurant seating and other products (mostly under the name "Plymold") publishes a month-to-date income statement every week. ECCO, an employee-owned Idaho company that makes backup alarms for trucks and "light bars" for police cars and other emergency vehicles, prepares a simplified income statement every week.[4] CPES holds monthly meetings at which team members review their performance so that they can make adjustments as necessary well before the end of a quarter.

Employees at these companies also learn to look forward—to forecast the key numbers. "When they get the financials [at the end of a month]," says Schramski of CPES employees, "they already know what's going to be in them . . . The whole idea is looking forward." Stack's open-book system creates, in effect, an ongoing three-part comparison, each part involving employees in managing the numbers from the ground up. One: a participatory budgeting process lays out the plan for the year. (At CPES the annual plan is known as the "stake in the ground.") Two: weekly, biweekly, or monthly financials show performance to date, compared with plan. Three: a weekly, biweekly, or monthly forecast shows how people think the *coming* period is shaping up—and thus allows them to make adjustments as necessary before something happens, rather than after.

The adjustments themselves, of course, are the nuts and bolts of frontline management. People figure out ways to bring in a little extra revenue or save a little more money this week. They plan for additional staffing because the next month is likely to be particularly busy. At King Arthur Flour's retail store, as we saw earlier, it's a matter of juggling daily sales dollars against daily labor hours. At Stone Construction Equipment, it's ensuring that labor time is allocated to the products that need to be built that day. At CPES, it's watching controllable expenses such as overtime hours and maintenance costs, week in and week out, and making decisions about how to manage those costs without compromising care.

This kind of responsibility transforms the meaning of "participative management" in an organization: now employees are participating directly in running their part of the company. Participation is no longer an "extra," it is an intrinsic part of the way the company operates. The meaning of accountability also undergoes a change. Like any employee, employee owners remain accountable for doing their individual jobs properly. But like any owner, they are now accountable for *the company's business results* as well. To be sure, the scope of accountability rises as you go up the hierarchy: only the CEO is accountable to the board for the entire organization's performance. But now it's not just executive vice presidents and division managers who are responsible for the performance of subunits; everyone in those subunits is accountable for whatever elements they can control. Thus team members at CPES are accountable for compiling their budget, for tracking their performance against budget, and for managing whatever they need to manage to hit (or better) the budgeted target. That is day-to-day business management in a nutshell, and the employee owners at equity companies learn to think and act like businesspeople—like partners in their enterprise.

REINFORCING THE MESSAGE

The open-book approach not only gets employee owners involved in running the day-to-day business, it also offers a way of cutting through some of the thorny problems that companies of all sorts regularly bump up against. Solving those problems in open-book fashion, moreover, reinforces the notion of employees as business partners. Consider just two examples.

One such problem is *incentive compensation.* "Incentive comp" is one of those carrots we mentioned earlier, and surely generates as much controversy (and uncertainty!) among employees and managers as any other facet of employment. Should we pay bonuses? How much, and to whom? How should the bonuses be determined? What will the bonus be this year? (And of course, "I wonder how much *her* bonus was compared with mine.") Open-book management may not end such controversies entirely, but it can eliminate the mystery and murk that surround most incentive-comp programs. Typically, open-book companies tie bonuses to achievement of specific business results over the course of a quarter or a year. They pay bonuses to everyone, usually as an equal percentage of salary or wages, because they operate on the assumption that everyone contributed to the results. Because people can see month in and month out how they are doing on those key performance measures, they can see whether they are likely to earn a bonus.

A bonus adds to whatever compensation may accrue to the employee owners—profit sharing, dividends, increased stock value—by virtue of their ownership. And of course, it is immediate, paid out in cash, which raises its visibility and impact. At CPES, for instance, the institution of a quarterly bonus tied to profit had a dramatic effect. "Suddenly a direct-care person earning $8 an hour was getting a check for $150 or $175," remembers Schramski. "Do you know what that was like to them? That was employee ownership! It just got people going . . . It really caught hold." Amy Rubinson, the supervisor, agrees that the bonus helped transform people's outlook:

> . . . The quarterly bonus system, I think people are really liking that. And everybody knows it's based on profit, so even if this home does great, it's the whole company [that counts]. And

> they're seeing, hey, we are getting this money, where the bonus
> system before, you were nominating people and it was really
> just not objective enough . . . everybody's really getting a piece
> of the pie this way. And my employees are definitely liking to
> get those envelopes every quarter. And [they] feel like the com-
> pany is really coming back down to the line staff and saying,
> "You're making this money for us. You're in there every day, in
> the housing, and we're going to recognize you for that."

In conventional companies, a bonus is in some sense artificial: it is
an inducement for employees to behave in a certain way so that shareholders will benefit. In equity companies, it is simply a graphic reminder that everybody is in this together and that everybody benefits
when the business succeeds.

A second problem: *initiatives*. Companies have launched so many
initiatives in recent years that some have dozens going simultaneously,
each with its task teams and rounds of meetings. By now the very word
is likely to elicit Dilbert-style eye-rolling. But the idea behind an initiative is simplicity itself: sometimes an organization needs to focus attention on a particular issue to achieve a definable result in a short time
frame. It needs to cut costs or boost quality in a given area. It needs to
learn a new skill. Troubles arise when initiatives are simply announced
from on high and when they bear no obvious relationship to the business disciplines that drive financial performance. Equity companies
practicing open-book management try not to make either mistake.
They get people involved from the beginning in designing their own
initiatives. They link the initiatives clearly to business results.

CPES, following Stack's vocabulary, refers to its initiatives as
"minigames." (The "big game," so to speak, is the game of business
itself.) In the huddle described earlier in the chapter, Bob Bennetti
reserved some time to report the results of the quarter's minigames.
Seven facilities won the vehicle-maintenance minigame—that is,
keeping the quarter's expenses below a certain level. Each staff member
at a winning facility got a coupon for a shopping trip. Stone Construction Equipment doesn't use the same vocabulary, but it does use the
same idea. When a particular work cell beats its labor-variance goal for

the month, as we mentioned in chapter 2, the managers cook the front-line employees a fancy meal.

We can't leave this topic without going back to those noisemakers and Silly String. How many companies would decide that a financial-review meeting is, well, an occasion for a good time? The mood at CPES's huddle was particularly festive: employees got a free lunch, a chance to let off some steam, and a chance to chat with people from around the company—all while carrying out the serious responsibility of reviewing their organization's performance. We talked about employee groups having fun in the previous chapter, but by and large it was off-site fun, at picnics and the like. CPES shows that work itself can be fun—even when the business at hand is serious.

8

Changing a Company

Thirty years ago, fewer than 2 million U.S. workers owned stock in the company that employed them. Today, the number is about 23 million, an increase of more than twelvefold in a period when the population increased by roughly 36 percent. Perhaps 10 million own options. Thirty years ago, employee ownership was almost completely unknown outside the United States, except for thriving but small cooperative sectors in Spain and Italy. Today, the United Kingdom, Australia, China, and many other countries have embarked upon programs designed to encourage employee ownership, and many of the largest U.S. and British multinationals routinely make stock available to their employees worldwide. So the simple act of sharing ownership has become almost commonplace. It is likely to become more so in the years to come.

The equity model, however—treating employee shareholders as true partners in enterprise, and operating the business in a way that reflects it—is far less common. Companies that offer stock to their employees often fail to challenge traditional assumptions and practices. They do little to change their culture. They make no effort to help employees think and act like businesspeople. This seems to us a waste. The research on employee ownership is unusually consistent and unusually clear: employee ownership boosts a company's performance, but only when it is combined with the kind of changes in culture and managerial style described in this book. Short of those changes, ownership is at best a nice benefit. At worst—a poorly designed plan in a badly managed or corrupt company—it can become a liability for everybody, as the people who once worked at Enron would be glad to testify.

So why hasn't the equity model spread farther? Why haven't more companies already taken advantage of this opportunity to improve performance and create more wealth?

Maybe it is only a question of time. The elements of the equity model described in this book were simply not a topic of anybody's conversation twenty years ago. Today they are. Attend any conference on employee ownership and you will hear extended discussions of ownership cultures, open-book management, and the other practices we have chronicled. We wrote this book to help speed along the process of information sharing. Like any human institution, business is governed partly by inertia and fear of change. Even in the best of circumstances, it would doubtless take a while—and probably a lot more books and conferences—before large numbers of companies seriously considered change of this magnitude.

And the circumstances aren't always the best. Some owners and executives—the people with the power to decide whether their companies take this course—will be personally uncomfortable with the equity model, whatever the theoretical appeal of higher profits and faster growth. To put it in pop-psychology terms, some of these business leaders have control issues. They think of the corporation as a machine—a race car, maybe—with themselves at the controls. Leaders who have spent long years scrambling to the top often arrive there with a deep devotion to this mechanical model and to the hierarchy it implies. One CEO, hearing a description of the high-involvement, low-hierarchy, participative style, bluntly told Martin Staubus, "Forget it! I didn't work my way up to become head of this company just to give up my executive parking space and have to go hide my Cadillac around the corner!" He may be more forthright than many of his peers, but he is probably not alone. Then, too, plenty of well-meaning leaders simply believe that hierarchy and control are the natural and proper order of things. People get promoted because of their skills and talents; these higher-skilled people should be charged with making more decisions.

Pushing decision making outward to employees—and especially to employee teams—might lead to chaos, or at least to decisions by people whose competence and interests are not appropriate to the matter at hand. As these leaders would (and do) put it, "a business is not a democracy." We, of course, aren't arguing that it is, but the model we are proposing raises such fears nonetheless.

Even for company leaders who *are* interested, the equity model is a tall order. It entails creating significant ownership programs and educating employees as to their meaning. It involves building a corporate culture that reinforces the message of ownership, ideally in a dozen different ways. And it means creating systems and structures that get employees involved in day-to-day business management, primarily through understanding and driving the numbers that determine a company's performance. Who should undertake such a journey? How and where would they start? Answering these questions—or at least suggesting the answers, because ultimately the answers must come from a company's leaders—is the job of this chapter.

WHO NEEDS EQUITY?

It isn't hard to justify employee ownership itself. Publicly traded companies may find that a broad-based options program or restricted-stock grants program, whatever the accounting rules, is a cost-effective means of adding to employee compensation and an essential tool of recruitment and retention. A 2003 study by Sibson Consulting found that, dollar for dollar, sharing ownership is the *most* effective way to lure employees to a new job or keep them at the one they have. In some industries employee ownership is already a competitive necessity. (Software and biotech are notable examples.) Closely held companies may find that an ESOP offers the owners tax-advantaged liquidity and provides employees with one piece of a valuable retirement plan.

So let's take the ownership piece for granted and ask the tougher question: under what circumstances does it make sense for an individual company to begin building an ownership culture and helping employees learn the disciplines that drive business performance? Companies in five categories seem particularly well suited to the process.

Destination Workplaces

Destination workplace is the phrase by which Green Mountain Coffee Roasters describes itself. But it can be applied to any company that offers employees good jobs, generous rewards, and a supportive environment. Companies in this category are already way ahead of the pack. They can often be found on the various "Best Companies to Work For" lists. A majority already have stock-ownership programs and a thriving, employee-centric culture. One of the newer exemplars is Google, the Internet search-engine firm that went public in 2004. Among other provisions of its unusual initial public offering (IPO), it announced that it would weight its stock so that its employee owners got ten times the votes of ordinary shareholders. (All "Googlers" have options and can buy stock in the company.) The company offers an extraordinary array of benefits, including free meals, on-site doctors, and washing machines. Most public companies come under pressure to decrease such lavish benefits; Google said it wants to *increase* them and created a voting structure likely to ensure that result. The company also allows employees 20 percent of their time to work on their own ideas. Larry Page, cofounder of the company, wrote in its IPO filing, "The significant employee ownership of Google has made us what we are today . . . Our main benefit is a workplace with important projects, where employees can contribute and grow. We are focused on providing an environment where talented, hard working people are rewarded for their contributions to Google and for making the world a better place."[1]

Companies with extraordinary benefits always run what might be called the Kodak risk. That is, they provide a great place to work until such time as they can no longer do so for business reasons—and when they cut back, employees are caught by surprise. It's astonishing to us that so many in this exclusive club do not take the logical next step and bring their employees into full partnership in the company, sharing information and getting them involved in running their parts of the business. The equity model offers them a chance to distance themselves further from the competition. It ties business logic to the generous benefits and positive culture they already provide. It may even help them avoid a situation where they abruptly have to shift into cost-cutting mode.

Southwest Airlines, a destination workplace if there ever was one, has begun moving in precisely this direction. For a few years now, Southwest has been faced with new competition, both from upstarts such as JetBlue Airways and AirTran Airways, and from the so-called legacy carriers such as American Airlines and Delta Air Lines, which have been dramatically reducing their costs. The company has made a decision to build upon its storied culture in exactly the ways portrayed in this book—that is, to help its employees learn to think and act like businesspeople. A "scoreboard" appearing regularly in the company's monthly employee magazine tracks and explains companywide financial results. Internal efforts are under way to help employees learn (and monitor) departmental performance metrics. Success in the airline industry today is more and more a matter of everyday decisions—whether pilots fly in a way that saves fuel, how fast ground personnel can turn planes around, whether employees overuse sick time, and so on. Southwest's employees are all shareholders, and they are learning what it means to act like owners day in and day out.

Companies Facing New and Potentially Devastating Competition

It is no secret: whole groups of American companies have simply vanished in the last couple of decades. Some have been forced out of business by imports. Other have been muscled aside by large, powerful competitors such as Wal-Mart or Home Depot. Still others have been undercut by younger, nimbler companies employing new technologies or business models. Employee ownership by itself is no protection against any of these competitive onslaughts. Weirton Steel, which succeeded for a while after an employee buyout, wound up in bankruptcy and was acquired by another steel company. By then, Weirton's workforce had shrunk to less than 25 percent of what it had been at the buyout (although even that was better than most of its competitors in the hard-hit steel industry). One of us (John Case) lives in a remodeled factory building near Boston; its previous occupant was a well-established employee-owned picture-frame manufacturer called M. W. Carr. The company was dissolved, and the Carr name sold off, in the mid-1990s, after its business had been devastated by imports.

The full equity model, by contrast, seems to give companies near-immunity against competitive threats. Thus Stone Construction Equipment has survived the wave of acquisitions and moves to Mexico that has plagued the rest of its industry; Jackson's Hardware has prospered under the very nose of Home Depot and Sears's Orchard Supply; W. L. Gore & Associates thrives as an American manufacturer thanks to its constant stream of associate-led innovation; and Phelps County Bank—a small community bank that competes with big national and statewide banks—has grown substantially and has periodically taken market share away from its larger competitors. "Our competition has increased tremendously," says Phelps CEO Bill Marshall. "The largest bank in the United States, Bank of America, is right across the street. But our market share has continued to hold or increase." The reasons for these companies' success are numerous, but many of them reflect the equity model: the companies are able to do things that their competitors can't, because of the deep involvement of their people in helping to drive the business. They are more innovative. Their employees care more about how customers are treated. True, there is no sure thing in business. But when a company is under brutal competitive assault, can it hurt to have hundreds or thousands of well-informed people, rather than just a few at the top, worrying about how the business can survive and prosper?

Companies Toiling in the Fields

Most companies, of course, are neither world-class destination workplaces nor in danger of being run out of business. They are more or less stable, middle-of-the-road enterprises just trying to grow and make money. The equity model is a way for them to distinguish themselves from all the other middle-of-the-road companies in their industry, because successfully implementing the model suddenly means that yours is no longer an ordinary business. Established in 1943, Building Material Distributors, Inc. (BMD) was a family-owned California company that sold to local markets. In 1991 it established an ESOP, and in 1995 it created a training program and an ESOP advisory team and began involving employees in helping to run the business. Today it has several branch offices throughout California and the Southwest, has hit more than $100 million in sales, and has begun to sell its building materials worldwide. BMD innovations, such as a particular kind of insulation panel for low-income housing, are used throughout the world. McKay Nursery Company, which traces its history back to 1897, might be just another small, rural company in a sleepy industry composed mostly of family-owned businesses. It isn't. Its challenges are not so much to grow as to pick and choose among growth opportunities, not so much to make money as to figure out how best to invest or distribute the sizable amounts of money it does make.

Young Growth-Oriented Companies

Young high-technology companies have long known the secret: the offer of equity is a great way to attract and keep high-quality people that a start-up couldn't otherwise afford. That's why broad-based option programs have been so popular in software and other technology-related businesses. (One young tech company in Virginia went so far as to christen itself TEOCO, The Employee Owned Company.) But plenty of nontech growth-oriented entrepreneurial businesses have discovered this secret. The Scooter Store, for example, based in Texas, sells power wheelchairs and electric scooters to elderly and disabled customers. Founded in 1991, it has since grown to more than $250 million in revenues and has made *Inc.* magazine's list of the five hundred fastest-growing privately held companies four times. Its one thousand one hundred employees own 40 percent of the company through an ESOP. When a young company such as the Scooter Store grows fast, its stock appreciates rapidly, and employees can build up huge account balances in a relatively short time. So ownership in a growth-oriented business of any sort can be a hugely attractive proposition.

Companies Whose Leaders Believe It's the Right Thing to Do

We have focused so far on the measurable benefits that the equity model offers all these companies: better productivity, more innovation, easier recruitment, higher rates of retention, and so forth. All these help a business succeed. But there is another kind of benefit that employee ownership provides, which is that it sets the company apart on an ethical level. According to pollster Daniel Yankelovich, 82 percent of consumers say it is "extremely important" that a company they do business with has "integrity" and "always deals honestly."[2] CPES overcame the mistrust facing a for-profit company in its industry when it became employee-owned and open-book. For young companies in particular, which have little or no track record to point to, employee ownership conveys the message that the founders are not in this just to make a quick buck.

Ethical considerations like these persuaded many companies to turn to employee ownership in the first place. An example is Allied Plywood, in Alexandria, Virginia. As we related in chapter 3, owner Ed Sanders could have sold his single-store, twenty-employee company to a large company for a respectable sum. But he wanted the employees to own the business they had helped build, so he sold to an ESOP instead. Twenty-four years later, Allied operates from multiple locations and is several times as big as it was when the ESOP began. Sanders is still proud of what he did: it was, he said, "just the right thing to do." Or take Starbucks. The company had a great business idea and no doubt could have been successful without giving everyone stock options and creating its own version of an equity-style culture. But CEO Howard Schultz didn't want employees to work for a company like the one that employed his father:

> I tried to make Starbucks the kind of company I wish my dad had worked for . . . Without even a high-school diploma, he probably could never have been an executive. But if he landed a job in one of our stores or roasting plants, he wouldn't have quit in frustration because the company didn't value him. He would have had great health benefits, stock options, and an atmosphere in which his suggestions and complaints would receive a prompt, respectful response . . . The bigger Starbucks grows, the more chance that some employee, somewhere, isn't getting the respect he or she deserves. If we can't attend to that problem, we are facing a failure worse than any shortcomings Wall Street can detect.[3]

Two of us (Corey Rosen and Martin Staubus) have spent decades talking to thousands of companies considering employee ownership. We have learned that the significance of ethical motives, and the benefits to those who act on them, should not be underestimated. While the equity model of business provides compelling competitive advantage, there is a human, ethical dimension involved in taking this road that for some may transcend the economic aspects.

Once it has taken root, moreover, the model creates a company less vulnerable to ethical abuses. Listen to John Cain, CEO of Scot Forge:

> I think one of the best things that have happened from being the CEO of an employee-owned company is—look, we have 485 employees. And I have 485 bosses! I feel accountable to every one of them. It's not a [situation in which] you feel like if you can just keep the board of directors happy, that is enough . . .
>
> My own personal belief is that I think everybody needs guidance. Everyone needs help. Everyone needs a boss. And I don't mean a boss in a way where you need somebody to micro-manage you. You need a good system of checks and balances. When you look at the corporate governance issues today, you look at some of the other choices people have made, that have cost their employees their company, and the lives and retirement that have been impacted by it, you can get insulated quite easily, and get surrounded by people that want to tell you it's the right thing to do, tell you ways to get away with it, rationalize it somehow. Not here; we are so transparent, we practice open-book management, and we operate on mutual trust. That rift is something that's not there . . . And there's an appreciation of the concept of a team of owners working together to build a company. It's more about how do you support that, how do you handle that, how the hell can you get out of the way to let them do what they do best? And don't get too enamored with ideas and concepts that take you away from those core fundamentals.

As Cain might suggest, there is one large group of companies that should avoid employee ownership entirely: companies whose leaders don't believe in the idea. Maybe this goes without saying. After all, the one factor common to all the businesses we studied, aside from their commitment to taking ownership seriously, is the passion the companies' founders and leaders brought to that commitment. Pursuing the equity model is a difficult enough journey for the committed. It is impossible for those who don't believe that it's worth doing.

HOW TO BEGIN

For a company that *is* committed, the obvious question is how to get started. We have carefully avoided offering any kind of blueprint for the process, just because it seems to us that companies do best when they find their own way. Certainly, the wide variety of organizations we visited chose unique paths and created unique versions of the equity model. W. L. Gore doesn't look much like SAIC. Neither one looks much like Jackson's Hardware or Stone Construction Equipment. The next exemplar that comes along, whether it is an established company undergoing a transformation or a growing young company that creates its own model, probably won't look like any of these.

That said, there are certain precepts that we're pretty sure the people we talked with would agree on. Most will be familiar from the other chapters in this book, but we will spell them out anyway, on the understanding that they are no more than guideposts.

Creating Ownership

Employee ownership is sufficiently common these days that, as we said, it isn't hard to create a plan. There are organizations, the National Center for Employee Ownership and the Beyster Institute among them, that can provide initial guidance. There are lawyers, consultants, and compensation experts who specialize in setting up workable plans. Companies with ESOPs have their own trade group, the ESOP Association. Professional staff at other equity compensation companies have the National Association of Stock Plan Professionals and even a certification program offered by the Certified Equity Professional Institute at Santa Clara University, in California. As far as ownership itself is concerned, the only critical points are that the plan be ample and that it be continuous. It must offer employees a chance to earn some real money over time if the company succeeds. It must include everybody, or nearly everybody (some plans exclude part-timers, for example). And it must provide an opportunity for the value of employees' ownership stakes to grow.

Education and Communication

Ownership is meaningless if employees don't know about it and don't understand what it means. As we argued elsewhere in the book, learning what it means takes time. Misconceptions must be overcome, basic information about the business shared. A point worth mentioning in this context is how little most Americans—and probably most people everywhere—learn about business in school. Several employee-owned companies have begun their business-literacy programs by asking employees to hazard a guess as to how many cents out of every sales dollar the company gets to keep in profit. Guesses often range from fifty cents upward, when of course the reality for most companies is that a dime out of every dollar is a healthy profit indeed. So information about the business has to be communicated simply and repeatedly. It's best done, moreover, not just in classes or in formal meetings but day in and day out, through scoreboards, through games and contests, and through simple financial statements that are updated monthly, weekly, or even daily.

Encouraging Involvement

An effective step toward successful employee participation is to set up a steering committee that includes both managers and frontline employees. Oddly, not every company takes this approach. Instead, management simply decides on the structures and procedures for employee participation. One can only wonder what employees make of this top-down approach to bottom-up involvement. A joint committee, by contrast, benefits from the clout of management's involvement and the credibility of employee representation. It is thus more likely to get buy-in from both sides. The committee can seek out ideas from other employee ownership companies, from books on employee participation (bookstore shelves groan with them), and from the many employee ownership and open-book management conferences. It also may want to survey employees and managers as to the state of things. We recommend asking blunt questions. What is the stupidest thing this company does? What is the one thing you need to do your job better? How would you rate the level of teamwork around here? What, from your point of view, is the biggest business challenge we're facing right now? A combination of general and very specific questions is likely to elicit a lot of information, probably including some surprising answers. Once the survey is complete, the committee can determine ways to get started—work teams, committees, and all the many other ideas we have already discussed.

This process may encounter two obstacles right at the outset. Some corporate leaders think they are committed to involvement when they are not. We're reminded of the time when one of us (Corey Rosen) visited a company in which the ESOP owned 30 percent of the stock. The founder was not thrilled with the ESOP; he thought employees didn't really appreciate it the way they should. At a meeting of senior managers, Corey went around the room and asked each person why he or she thought that was the case. Without exception, they replied, "It's you, Charlie"—referring to the CEO. (Charlie is not his real name.) "You ask people for ideas, but you never really listen." Michael Keeling, of the ESOP Association, recounts a similar experience in visiting another ESOP company:

> I'm down at the company, and they're having me join their ESOP employee committee meeting. They're going down their agenda, and the CEO is sitting not at the table but on the couch at the side. He pipes in every now and then and gives his opinion, and they go back and forth.
>
> Then they get to the item on the agenda where the question is, are they going to spend $1,500 to sponsor something on the local public radio station. Some children's show or whatever. They had spent $750 and got thirty minutes [before], and the station called in and said, now you have to buy an hour, and you're going to have to pay $1,400 or something. And so the men and women at the table were kind of like, well, you know, this is what we do for the community, and they were reluctantly saying, this is what we do, it's OK and so forth. And then all of a sudden the CEO pipes up and he says, "Aw, this is too big of an increase. This is one I think we ought to skip this year." And the whole group, nobody opened their mouth! They immediately dropped it. And I [said to the CEO], "I love you, but don't you realize you just basically countermanded all your employees? Let 'em make a decision!"

So part of a company leader's job is to encourage the formation of employee groups. The other part is to shut up and let these groups make decisions.

A second obstacle is likely to come from middle management. Middle managers are often the forgotten men and women of change initiatives. Frontline employees get the attention. Frontline employees are supposed to be the ones coming up with the ideas and taking control of their work situation. Middle managers are not only overlooked, they may be deliberately undermined. Not surprisingly, they do their best to ignore or sabotage whatever orders are coming down from above. Involvement? Sure, we'll do involvement, so long as it's on our terms. In the equity model, of course, middle managers have a huge role to play, but it's as leaders and coaches more than as order givers. The challenge for senior executives is to help those middle managers who can adapt do so, and to find other roles for those who cannot. Eventually, some of the latter group are likely to leave.

Learning and Driving the Business

The hardest step of all is helping employees learn the business disciplines that are essential to a company's success, and then incorporating their involvement into the daily management of the company. More how-to information is available from books on open-book management, particularly Jack Stack's and Bo Burlingham's *The Great Game of Business* and John Case's *Open-Book Management: The Coming Business Revolution*. Again, there are consultants specializing in open-book management who can help a company get started. But at the risk of oversimplifying, let us lay out a five-part process for this critical step:

- *Identify your critical number(s).* This by itself is a process of employee involvement. What do they think are the critical challenges facing their part of the business right now? Improving productivity? Boosting sales? Getting a new product out the door? Reducing backlog? Getting control of inventory? The list of possibilities is long, but any one company shouldn't have trouble homing in on a small number of likely candidates. Then ask the same question of management, to see if the priorities are the same. Finally, check the top candidates against external indicators, such as the financial statements and an assessment of the marketplace. The *process* of coming to agreement is critically important, because what you want is for everyone to buy in: yes, this is the one number (or two, or whatever) that needs to improve if we are to "win the business game" this year.

- *Set a target.* Numbers are rarely meaningful except in relation to one another. A 12 percent operating margin in any given year might be great for some companies, but it's pretty bad for a company that enjoyed 18 percent last year. So, given that we want to improve on metric X, the question now is, by how much? *The target shouldn't be a shot in the dark.* Rather, it should be based on a hard-nosed assessment of what is possible and why. Sales will go up because we expect to add a certain number of new customers, and here is what we are doing to find them. Shipments will rise because the economy is turning around, and here is the evidence from our industry to support it. Again, however, the point is to get buy-in to the goal. Edicts handed down from on high won't have the desired effects.

- *Gather ideas about how to move the needle.* This is the kind of employee involvement that should continue day in and day out. Here is the goal—now what needs to happen so that we improve our chances of reaching it? In most companies, employees immediately realize what they don't know. Did that improvement we made last year really make a difference? Can we save money by sending that process out instead of doing it in house? So, first comes data gathering—but data gathering then typically leads to experimentation, and experimentation to improvement.

- *Monitor and track the critical numbers.* We wrote in chapter 7 about the importance of "scoreboards" of some sort. We have seen companies where the entire wall of the lunchroom is covered in big numbers. We have seen others that put out a little dashboard-style or instrument-panel gauge on everybody's computer. You can't play the game effectively unless you know if you're winning or losing. (And it isn't much fun anyway.)

- *Celebrate and reward "wins."* An annual goal necessarily breaks down into quarterly and monthly (and in some companies, weekly or daily) goals. When you reach one, pause to note that fact. Treat people to lunch on the company. Hand out movie tickets. Discuss pegging your bonus plan to attainment of the critical numbers, with quarterly payouts that start small and build up near the end of the year.

The sequence of these steps is not critical, except in obvious cases. (You can't celebrate wins until you know that you have won.) Some companies begin involving employees in running the business even before they have established an ownership plan. Many have already started with the ownership plan, but haven't yet taken the next steps toward the full equity model. What is important is that you make a plan, start it, and stick to it.

We would add one final word. We have described a model of business in this book that we have repeatedly said is difficult to implement. We know it is difficult because we have watched companies do it. On the other hand, pretty much anything worth doing in business these days is hard. We are all in the midst of a series of extended changes: globalization, the information revolution, the rearrangement and restructuring of all sorts of industries. The question isn't whether a new way of running a company is hard to implement—of course it will be—but whether it is better suited to the challenges of the twenty-first century than the old way of doing things. We believe that the equity model passes this test with flying colors. Businesses that would otherwise have gone under, such as Stone and Jackson's Hardware, survive. Businesses such as SAIC, Southwest Airlines, and W. L. Gore grow into market leaders. Businesses such as Scot Forge and McKay Nursery Company merely continue to pile up the profits year after year and to provide a *very* comfortable financial cushion for the people who work there—just as Louis Kelso might have hoped.

This is no small accomplishment. But there's something else to be said for pursuing the equity model as well. Too many businesses—too many workplaces—support a kind of humdrum existence. People go to work, collect their paychecks, and go home. There is little sense of purpose, of meaning, of engagement and involvement, of ambition to make things better. Creating a company that is owned by its employees—one that takes that ownership seriously—is, not to put too fine a point on it, a heroic cause, an objective that makes it worthwhile to get up in the morning and go to work.

We have relied on the employee owners we spoke with to make many of our points in this book, and it seems only fitting that we give them the last word. So listen to three different voices, and ask yourself whether it wouldn't be pretty great to run a company and provide an environment that people felt this way about:

> Employee ownership is very important. Very important. First of all it's the stock that I'm putting aside for my retirement . . . But the second part, which is probably just as important, is the feeling of camaraderie. We're all working for ourselves. And so everybody really puts in more than the minimum, more than they have to. Everybody is really concerned that the company does make money, that we do our best to keep our costs down. Just working in that kind of atmosphere . . .
>
> It would be really great if every worker in this country could be part of an employee-owned company. That would just be awesome. I think it's one of the only ways that everyday working people can get hold of true wealth. It's the greatest thing in the world.
>
> —Karen York, staff accountant, Scot Forge

> I love it! Oh, my god! I worked at a large health-care facility with five thousand employees for seventeen years. I was the office manager . . . The difference between working there for seventeen years and working here is like night and day. The differences are that here, people really care about what you have to say. Granted, it's a lot smaller company, so it's a lot easier to be heard than it is at the hospital . . . [But] here, I feel I can see where my work goes, and everybody is working for the same thing. We're all employee owners, we know that there's profit sharing at the end, we know that working together is important, and we're all trying to participate in getting the results at the end.
>
> —Sherry Ceresa, statistical analyst, Gardener's Supply

I would have to say personally it gives me more of a commit-ment to my job. As well as pride. More individual ties, when we're struggling and when we're successful. It's not them and me, it's us . . .

I think the atmosphere and the value and pride we have in our company makes people want to be here. They're part of something. It gives you a good feeling of purpose in life.

—Cindy Ferguson, manufacturing associate,
    life sciences product group, YSI

Plans for Broad-Based Employee Ownership

The following is a listing of the various methods by which U.S. companies can provide stock to their employees.

An *employee stock ownership plan (ESOP)* is a type of tax-qualified employee benefit plan in which most or all of the plan's assets are invested in stock of the employer. Like profit-sharing and 401(k) plans, which are governed by many of the same laws, an ESOP generally must include all full-time employees meeting certain age and service requirements. Employees do not actually buy shares in an ESOP. Instead, the company contributes its own shares to the plan, contributes cash that the ESOP can use to buy its own stock (often from an existing owner), or, most commonly, has the plan borrow money to buy stock, with the company repaying the loan. All of these uses offer significant tax benefits for the company, the employees, and the sellers. Employees who become vested in their accounts receive their benefits when they leave the company (although there may be distributions before that). More than 8 million employees in eleven thousand–plus companies, mostly closely held, participate in ESOPs.

A *stock option plan* grants employees the right—once the option has vested—to buy company stock at a specified price during a specified period. So if an employee gets an option on one hundred shares at $10 and the stock price goes up to $20, the employee can "exercise" the option: buy those one hundred shares at $10 each, sell them on the market for $20 each, and pocket the difference. If the stock price never rises above the option price, the employee will simply not exercise the option. Stock options can be given to as many or as few employees as a company wishes. An estimated 7 to 10 million employees—possibly more—presently hold stock options; these employees work for thousands of different companies, both public and private.

Restricted stock plans provide employees with shares, or with the right to buy shares at fair market value or at a discount. However, the shares employees acquire are subject to a vesting restriction. The most common restriction is that the employee must continue to work for the company for a certain length of time, typically three to five years; if the employee leaves the company earlier, the shares are forfeited back to the company. The time-based restrictions may pass all at once or gradually. Other kinds of restrictions may be imposed, however. The company can, for instance, restrict the shares until certain business performance goals are achieved. With restricted stock units (RSUs), employees do not actually receive shares *until* the restrictions lapse.

A *qualified employee stock purchase plan (ESPP)* is a little like a stock option plan. As spelled out in rules prescribed in the Internal Revenue Code, it gives employees the chance to buy stock, usually through payroll deductions over a three-month to twenty-seven-month "offering period." The price may be discounted up to 15 percent from the market price. Frequently, employees can choose to buy stock at a discount from the lower of either the price at the beginning or the price at the end of the ESPP offering period, which can increase the discount still further. As with a stock option, after acquiring the stock the employee can sell it for a quick profit or hold on to it. Unlike with stock options, the discounted price built into most ESPPs means that employees can profit even if the stock price has gone down since the grant date. Under the rules for these tax-qualified "Section 423" plans, almost all full-time employees with two years or more of service must be allowed to participate (although in practice, many choose not to). Many millions of employees, almost always in public companies, are in ESPPs.

A *nonqualified employee stock purchase plan* is, quite simply, a program by which a company sells shares of its stock to its employees without regard to the qualification rules that are prescribed by law for ESPPs (described earlier). Many companies, especially those that are not publicly traded, find it impractical or undesirable to sell stock to employees under the terms prescribed for ESPPs. Companies are free to sell stock to employees without following those rules, the trade-off being a loss of certain favorable tax provisions for employee purchasers. Any sales of stock to an employee by a privately held company must comply with the restrictions imposed by federal and state securities laws.

A *Section 401(k) plan*, usually known just as a 401(k), is a retirement plan that, unlike an ESOP, is designed to provide the employee with a diversified portfolio of investments. Like an ESOP, however, a 401(k) plan is a tax-qualified plan that generally must include all full-time employees meeting age and service requirements. The employees can choose among several or more choices for investments, and the company may make a matching contribution. Perhaps several million employees in a few thousand companies participate in plans with a heavy company stock component; company stock may be an investment choice for the employees, the means by which the company makes matching contributions, or both. The plans may be combined with ESOPs—these are called "KSOPs"—where the company match is an ESOP contribution.

Stock appreciation rights plans provide employees with a payout, usually in cash but sometimes in shares of stock, based on the increase in the company's stock value during a particular period of time. Essentially, they offer employees a bonus based on the company's stock performance. An emerging variant on stock appreciation rights is the notion of "stock settled stock appreciation rights" (SS-SARs), which are appreciation rights settled in shares instead of cash. SS-SARs are less dilutive than stock options, but otherwise are essentially the same as nonqualified options in terms of taxes and accounting. Stock appreciation rights and phantom-stock plans that pay out cash instead of shares may be simpler than programs that provide actual shares, but they may not provide the same sense of ownership that share-based plans do.

Chapter 1

1. Any direct quotation unaccompanied by a note comes from personal communication with one of the authors.

2. Data from the National Center for Employee Ownership and authors' research. On the Lusty Lady, see Tad Friend, "Naked Profits," *New Yorker*, July 12 and 19, 2004, 56.

3. Estimate provided by professor Joseph Blasi of Rutgers, The State University of New Jersey. Blasi has examined public records relating to P&G's benefit plans and confirms from this source that the company is at least 10 percent employee owned. He estimates that additional share ownership from the company's international employee ownership programs, employee use of other investment plans, and direct ownership by employees and retirees adds up to another 5 to 10 percent of outstanding shares.

4. Douglas Kruse, "Statement for the Senate Roundtable on 'Preserving *Partnership Capitalism* Through Stock Options for America's Workforce,'" unpublished, May 8, 2003.

5. National Center for Employee Ownership, "A Statistical Profile of Employee Ownership," updated 2003, http://www.nceo.org.

6. David Dorsey, "Happiness Pays," *Inc.*, February 2004, 91.

7. "Robert Shillman: Making Machine Vision a Reality," *Fortune*, March 8, 2004, 190[L].

8. See William Greider, *The Soul of Capitalism* (New York: Simon & Schuster, 2003), 145–152.

9. Douglas Kruse, "Research Evidence on Prevalence and Effects of Employee Ownership," testimony before the Subcommittee on Employer-Employee Relations, Committee on Education and the Workforce, U.S. House of Representatives, February 13, 2002.

10. Douglas Kruse, Joseph Blasi, Jim Sesil, and Maya Krumova, "Broadly

Granted Stock Options Improve Corporate Performance," in *Employee Ownership and Corporate Performance* (Oakland, CA: National Center for Employee Ownership, 2004).

11. Kruse, "Statement for the Senate Roundtable." For those who doubt Kruse's academic integrity and thus his conclusions because he is a well-known advocate of employee ownership, we hasten to add that a good portion of the studies were conducted by very-much-mainstream researchers. For example, the consulting firm Hewitt Associates and Northwestern University's Kellogg Graduate School of Management carried out a study in 1999 of some 380 companies. The researchers unambiguously concluded, "Companies that adopt employee stock ownership plans (ESOPs) readily outpace their industry peers in financial performance." Hewitt Associates, "Unleashing the Power of Employee Ownership," April 1999.

12. "Testimony of Craig Barrett, CEO of Intel Corporation," House Committee on Financial Services, Subcommittee on Capital Markets, Insurance and Government-Sponsored Enterprises, U.S. House of Representatives, June 3, 2003.

13. National Center for Employee Ownership, "Employee Ownership Update," May 5, 2004.

14. "On the Record: John Chambers," *San Francisco Chronicle*, February 29, 2004.

15. Andy Serwer, "Hot Starbucks to Go," *Fortune*, January 26, 2004, 70.

16. Bruce Bartlett, "The Myth of Employee Ownership" (Washington, DC: National Center for Policy Analysis, December 5, 2002).

17. Joseph Blasi, Douglas Kruse, and Aaron Bernstein, *In the Company of Owners* (New York: Basic Books, 2003).

18. Note that what's at issue here is only *reported* earnings—that is, net profit as determined by accounting standards. Changing an accounting standard has no effect on the amount of cash a company actually takes in.

19. John Leland, "Putting All the Nest Eggs in the Company Basket," *New York Times*, April 11, 2004.

Chapter 2

1. This account draws on personal interviews and on Tammy Mitchell, "People Power: The Transformation of Stone Construction Equipment" (Albany, NY: Empire State Development, 1995).

2. Laird Harrison, "We're All the Boss," *Time* Bonus Section: Inside Business, April 2002.

3. Brad Bartholomew, "Believing in the SWA Model," unpublished, September 1, 2002.

4. See John Case, "The Power of Listening," *Inc.*, March 2003, 81. Atlas is not employee owned, but it has a so-called phantom-stock plan, in which employees could buy stock appreciation rights through a payroll deduction (see the appendix). Most had taken advantage of this plan, which would pay them the value of their "shares" when they retired or when the business was sold.

Chapter 3

1. Robert G. Sherrill, "Louis Kelso: Nut or Newton?" *The Nation*, March 2, 1970, 235.

2. Louis O. Kelso and Patricia Hetter Kelso, "Why I Invented the ESOP LBO," *Leaders* 12, no. 4 (October, November, December 1989): 76.

3. Stuart M. Speiser, *A Piece of the Action* (New York: Van Nostrand Reinhold Co., 1977), 129. Speiser was a lawyer specializing in airplane disaster litigation who got excited about Kelso's work, talked to him extensively, and wrote this book with considerable help from Jeff Gates. Our account draws heavily on it.

4. "Labor's Untapped Wealth," an address delivered by Louis O. Kelso at the Air Line Pilots Association Retirement and Insurance Seminar, March 1984, Washington, DC. Available from the Kelso Institute, http://www.kelso institute.org/lectures.html.

5. Speiser, *A Piece of the Action*, 137.

6. Louis O. Kelso and Mortimer J. Adler, *The Capitalist Manifesto* (repr., Westport, CT: Greenwood Press, 1975), 216. Page number refers to the reprint edition.

7. Ibid., 71.

8. Ibid., 219.

9. Ibid., 249.

10. From here on, we will refer to "Kelso's" ideas rather than "Kelso's and Adler's." Though *The Capitalist Manifesto* was written by both men, the fundamental ideas were all Kelso's, as Adler was quick to acknowledge in his introduction to the book.

11. Steve Leikin, "The Citizen Producer: The Rise and Fall of Working-Class Cooperatives in the United States," in *Consumers Against Capitalism? Consumer Cooperation in Europe, North America, and Japan, 1840–1990*, ed. Ellen Furlough and Carl Strikwerda (Lanham, MD: Rowman & Littlefield, 1999). Chapter retrieved in manuscript form, April 22, 2004, http://www.wisc .edu/uwcc/info/history/citizen_producer.pdf; quotation from pp. 10 and 12.

12. "The World of Co-Operation," *Economist*, May 3, 1975.

13. Richard Donkin, *Blood, Sweat, and Tears: The Evolution of Work* (New York and London: Texere LLC, 2001), 264. It should be noted that there is a

continuing debate among partisans of co-ops about the extent to which Mondragón has compromised its co-op principles in order to succeed as a business—for example, by hiring nonowning workers in some of its facilities. See George Cheney, *Values at Work: Employee Participation Meets Market Pressure at Mondragón* (Ithaca, NY: Cornell University Press, 1999).

14. Raymond Russell, Art Hochner, and Stewart E. Perry, "San Francisco's 'Scavengers' Run Their Own Firm," *Working Papers for a New Society* 2, no. 2 (Summer 1977): 32.

15. Leland Stanford, "Co-operation of Labor," *New York Tribune*, May 4, 1887. Special Collection 33a, Box 7, Folder 74, Stanford University Archives. Cited in Lee Altenberg, "Beyond Capitalism: Leland Stanford's Forgotten Vision," *Sandstone and Tile* 14, no. 1 (Winter 1990): 8–20.

16. The examples and figures are drawn from the fine account in Joseph Blasi, Douglas Kruse, and Aaron Bernstein, *In the Company of Owners* (New York: Basic Books, 2003), 162–164. See also the examples cited in John Calder, *Modern Industrial Relations* (New York: Longmans, Green and Co., 1924).

17. Josephine Young Case and Everett Needham Case, *Owen D. Young and American Enterprise* (Boston: David R. Godine, 1982), 374.

18. "Life of Owen D. Young," *Fortune*, February 1931, 111.

19. Sumner Slichter, "The Current Labor Policies of American Industries," *Quarterly Journal of Economics* 43, no. 2 (May 1929): 409.

20. Case and Case, *Owen D. Young*, 375.

21. Robert Bussel, "'Business Without a Boss': The Columbia Conserve Company and Workers' Control, 1917–1943," *Business History Review* 71, no. 3 (Autumn 1997): 417–443.

22. This account mainly follows Kelso's lecture, "Labor's Untapped Wealth," March 1984, Washington, DC. It also draws on the account in Speiser, *A Piece of the Action*, 163–165. There are minor disparities between the two: for example, Kelso says the events took place in 1955, Speiser in 1956.

23. Speiser, *A Piece of the Action*, 164.

24. Ibid., 156.

25. This account is based on Speiser, *A Piece of the Action*, 191–195, on an interview with Norman Kurland, and on the videotape of an introduction of Sen. Long by Wayne Thevenot to the ESOP Association, 1986.

26. Speiser, *A Piece of the Action*, 193.

27. Ibid., 205.

28. See the list of 1970s and 1980s legislation in Joseph Blasi, *Employee Ownership: Revolution or Ripoff?* (Cambridge, MA: Ballinger Publishing Co., 1988), 33–35. Blasi notes that "in 1986 Chrysler workers sold back most of their stock to the company, indicating that both Chrysler and the union

viewed employee ownership only as a temporary part of the company's re-vival." But the workers made money on the deal—more than they had to give up in wages. Later, Chrysler boss Lee Iacocca said in his best-selling book that he had created the ESOP, when in fact he had opposed it.

29. See the excellent history of stock options in Blasi, Kruse, and Bern-stein, *A Company of Owners*.

30. An option is a right to buy a company's stock at a given price. If you get an option at $20, your option is worthless unless and until the stock goes above $20. When the stock price is below $20, the option is said to be "under water."

31. For example, Michael Grund and Richard Ericson, of the human resources consulting firm Towers Perrin, examined the stock prices of 350 companies that announced they would voluntarily expense option grants. The prices of these companies' shares showed no significant variation in comparison with similar companies that were not expensing options. See Corey Rosen, "Learning to Live Profitably with Expensing," *Wall Street Journal*, July 20, 2004.

Chapter 4

1. The newspaper ran a four-part series on United's travails from July 13 through July 16. The quote from the mechanic in the previous paragraph and the examples of new behavior are taken from the second installment, "ESOP's Fable Forces Airline to Brink," July 14, 2003.

2. Roger Lowenstein, "Into Thin Air," *New York Times Magazine*, February 17, 2002, 43–44.

3. Lowenstein, "Into Thin Air," 44. The examples in this paragraph are taken from Lowenstein, the figures regarding on-time performance from the *Chicago Tribune* series.

4. "Summer of Hell Exacts Heavy Toll," *Chicago Tribune*, July 15, 2003.

5. Christopher Mackin, "United It Was Not," January 2003, Ownership Associates, Inc., http://www.ownershipassociates.com.

6. Lowenstein, "Into Thin Air," 44.

7. Cited in Philippa Strum, *Brandeis: Beyond Progressivism* (Lawrence, KS: University Press of Kansas, 1993), 37.

8. Much later—in the 1980s—Dan River was owned by its employees through an ESOP for a period of years.

9. Department of Manufacturing, Chamber of Commerce of the United States, "Employee Representation or Works Councils" (Washington, DC: Chamber of Commerce of the United States, June 1927), 15–17.

10. John Case, "A More Perfect Union," *Audacity*, Fall 1993, 62.

11. Cited in ibid.

12. Ben M. Selekman, *Sharing Management with the Workers* (New York: Russell Sage Foundation, 1924), xiii.

13. Sanford M. Jacoby, *Modern Manors: Welfare Capitalism Since the New Deal* (Princeton, NJ: Princeton University Press, 1997), 13.

14. Ibid., 69.

15. Ibid., 61.

16. Ibid., 62.

17. Ibid., 80.

18. Ibid., 85.

19. Ibid., 93.

20. Ben Rand, "Loosening the Kodak Ties That Bind," *Democrat and Chronicle* (Rochester, NY), December 14, 2003.

21. Andrea Gabor, *The Capitalist Philosophers* (New York: Times Business, 2000), 113. Gabor's account of the human relations school—told in a chapter on Roethlisberger and Mayo and another on Maslow and McGregor—is one of the best we have seen.

22. Paul Blumberg, *Industrial Democracy: The Sociology of Participation* (New York: Schocken Books, 1969), 24–26.

23. See Robert H. Guest, "Quality of Work Life—Learning from Tarrytown," *Harvard Business Review*, July–August 1979, 76–87. Guest defines QWL, as it was known, as "a *process* by which an organization attempts to unlock the creative potential of its people by involving them in decisions affecting their work lives."

24. Peter Drucker, *The Practice of Management* (New York: Harper & Row, 1954; New York: Perennial Library, 1986), 306–307. Page numbers refer to the Perennial Library edition.

25. Cited in John Simmons and William Mares, *Working Together: Employee Participation in Action* (New York: New York University Press, 1982, 1985 paperback), 194.

26. Gabor, *The Capitalist Philosophers*, 182.

27. Eileen Appelbaum, Thomas Bailey, and Peter Berg, *Manufacturing Advantage: Why High-Performance Work Systems Pay Off* (Ithaca, NY, and London: Cornell University Press, 2000), 57.

28. Art Kleiner, "Management Bites Dog Food Factory," *Fast Company*, June/July 1996, 44.

29. Richard Donkin, *Blood, Sweat & Tears* (New York and London: Texere, 2001), 243.

30. See Frits K. Pil and John Paul MacDuffie, "Organizational and Environmental Factors Influencing the Use and Diffusion of High-Involvement

Work Practices," in *Employment Practices and Business Strategy*, ed. Peter Cappelli (New York: Oxford University Press, 1999).

31. Stanley Holmes, "Boeing: Putting Out the Labor Fires," *BusinessWeek*, December 29, 2003, 43.

32. Gabor, *The Capitalist Philosophers*, 182.

33. Ibid., 172–173.

34. See Gilbert S. Krulee, "Remembering Joe Scanlon," May 9, 2004, http://www.scanlonleader.org/Scanlon/ScanlonWebSite/home.html. Krulee worked as a graduate assistant to Scanlon in 1947.

35. See, for example, *Fortune* magazine, eds., *Working Smarter* (New York: Viking Press, 1982), 112–113.

36. Timothy Aeppel, "Tricks of the Trade: On Factory Floors, Top Workers Hide Secrets to Success," *Wall Street Journal*, July 1, 2002.

37. Cited in Gabor, *The Capitalist Philosophers*, 79.

38. Thomas J. Peters and Robert H. Waterman Jr., *In Search of Excellence: Lessons from America's Best-Run Companies* (New York: Warner Books, 1982), 75.

39. Terrence E. Deal and Allan A. Kennedy, *Corporate Cultures: The Rites and Rituals of Corporate Life* (Reading, MA: Addison-Wesley Publishing Co., 1982).

40. Walton's autobiography is Sam Walton, *Made in America*, with John Huey (New York: Bantam Books, 1993). This quote is from Mark Gimein, "Sam Walton Made Us a Promise," *Fortune*, March 18, 2002, 123.

41. Walton, *Made in America*, 206.

42. Gimein, "Sam Walton Made Us a Promise," 122.

43. Robert Slater, *The Wal-Mart Decade* (New York: Portfolio, 2003), 52.

44. Gimein, "Sam Walton Made Us a Promise," 128.

45. "Store Wars," first aired August 28, 2001. See http://www.pbs.org/itvs/storewars/.

46. Jack Stack and Bo Burlingham, *A Stake in the Outcome: Building a Culture of Ownership for the Long-Term Success of Your Business* (New York: Doubleday/Currency, 2002), 102. See also Jack Stack, *The Great Game of Business*, with Bo Burlingham (New York: Doubleday/Currency, 1992).

47. John Case, "The Open-Book Managers," *Inc.*, September 1990.

48. John Case, *Open-Book Management: The Coming Business Revolution* (New York: HarperBusiness, 1995); John Case, *The Open-Book Experience* (Reading, MA: Perseus Books, 1998).

49. Jody Hoffer Gittell, *The Southwest Airlines Way* (New York: McGraw-Hill, 2003), 6.

50. Kevin and Jackie Freiberg, *Nuts! Southwest Airlines' Crazy Recipe for Business and Personal Success* (New York: Broadway Books, 1996), 121.

51. Ibid., 88.

Chapter 5

1. Biographical details from company materials and published reports, including Carolyn T. Geer, "Turning Employees into Stakeholders," *Forbes*, December 1, 1997, 155.

2. Debra Sherman, "In Their Own Words, Part II: Five Winning Commentaries," *Leading Companies E-Zine*, April 2003, http://www.beysterinstitute.org/onlinemag/apr03/culture.htm.

3. Corey M. Rosen, Katherine J. Klein, and Karen M. Young, *Employee Ownership in America: The Equity Solution* (Lexington, MA: Lexington Books, 1986), 124.

4. SG&A refers to sales, general, and administrative expenses.

5. EBITDA refers to earnings before interest, taxes, depreciation, and amortization. It is a measure of a company's operating cash flow.

6. Of course, any closely held company has an implicit repurchase obligation; otherwise, no one would want to own its shares. Imagine a family business, for example, in which one of the shareholding cousins wants to cash out of the company. The money to buy his or her shares has to come from somewhere, and it's typically the company's own cash.

Like any owner, an ESOP can realize its obligation to the shareholders by buying them out with the company's cash, by selling the company, or by going public. It's just that ESOPs are the only owners that are required to meet their repurchase obligation on a defined schedule—that is, when each shareholder leaves the company.

Chapter 6

1. See Rick Carter, "W. L. Gore & Associates, Inc.: Quality's Different Drummer," *Industrial Maintenance & Plant Operation*, October 2003.

2. Milestones compiled from company documents.

3. Ann Harrington, "Who's Afraid of a New Product?" *Fortune*, November 10, 2003, 189. See also Alan Deutschman, "The Fabric of Creativity," *Fast Company*, December 2004, 53–62. "Pound for pound," says Deutschman, "the most innovative company in America is W. L. Gore & Associates."

4. The principles are taken from the company's Web site, http://www.gore.com/about/culture.html.

5. Barbara Ehrenreich, *Nickel and Dimed: On (Not) Getting By in America* (New York: Henry Holt & Co., 2001).

6. For an account of the workplace hardships of white-collar employees, most of them very well paid, see Jill Andresky Fraser, *White-Collar Sweatshop: The Deterioration of Work and Its Rewards in Corporate America* (New York: W. W. Norton & Co., 2001).

7. Charles Fishman, "The Anarchist's Cookbook," *Fast Company*, July 2004, available at http://www.fastcompany.com/magazine/84/wholefoods.html. Publicly traded Whole Foods Market has a broad-based options program—94 percent of outstanding options are held by nonexecutive employees—and an employee stock purchase plan.

8. Ibid., 70.

9. Ron Lieber, "New Way to Curb Medical Costs: Make Employees Feel the Sting," *Wall Street Journal*, June 23, 2004.

10. Kevin and Jackie Freiberg, *Nuts! Southwest Airlines' Crazy Recipe for Business and Personal Success* (New York: Broadway Books, 1996), 115.

Chapter 7

1. Tom Schramski left the company in 2004. When he departed, CPES was required to rename itself; in Arizona, no company without a licensed psychologist can include the word "psychology" in its name, and Schramski was the only licensed psychologist on the payroll.

2. Kevin and Jackie Freiberg, *Nuts! Southwest Airlines' Crazy Recipe for Business and Personal Success* (New York: Broadway Books, 1996), 58–59.

3. GED stands for general equivalency diploma; it usually means that the holder didn't finish a regular high school program but instead completed high school requirements later.

4. See John Case, *The Open-Book Experience* (Reading, MA: Perseus Books, 1998), 37.

Chapter 8

1. "Letter from the Founders: 'An Owner's Manual' for Google's Shareholders," included in Google's S-1 filing to the Securities and Exchange Commission, April 29, 2004.

2. Speech at NCEO conference, March 27, 2003.

3. Howard Schultz, *Pour Your Heart into It* (New York: Hyperion, 1997).

ACKNOWLEDGMENTS

Over twenty-five years of working in the field of employee ownership, I have accumulated an entire book's length of people I should thank for making this all possible. Since I can't thank everyone, I'll simply acknowledge that the enormous growth of this concept has been the result of exceptional contributions by literally millions of people. There are academics who studied it, values-driven professionals who implemented the plans, legislators who, despite the lack of political incentives, pushed the ideas just because they thought they were right, and business leaders who believed that treating people with dignity and respect was actually the best business model they could choose. Even more important, there were millions of employee owners who actually made this happen through their own hard work and ideas. It's their stories that give all of us active in this field both a reason to keep going and something worthwhile to talk about. Of course, there are also friends and family, who have so enriched my life outside of employee ownership.

Still, there are a few people I want to single out. Louis Kelso, the father of ESOPs, devoted his life to an idea that for decades was generally regarded as at best eccentric and at worst absurd. But he persevered and, in the end, made us all better off for it. My friends and coconspirators Joseph Blasi and Doug Kruse at Rutgers have doggedly pursued the data on broad-based ownership for twenty-five years, compiling academically acclaimed research that has been absolutely essential to the growth of this idea. Members of the National Center for Employee Ownership (NCEO) board, all volunteers serving at their own expense, have been a great source of support and ideas. The staff of the NCEO, now and over the last twenty-three years, has been remarkable. They have brought a level of intelligence, dedication, creativity, and determination that has allowed me to be mostly their colleague and rarely their boss. I especially want to thank those who worked here more than ten years: Scott Rodrick, Eimear Elzy (both still with us), and, especially, Karen Young, who cofounded the Center with me in 1981 and who, for the next twelve years, did almost everything there was to do here. Michael Quarrey, one of our first staff members and now a board member, has been a stalwart friend and endless source of feedback and great ideas.

As essential as all these people have been, I am dedicating this book to William Foote Whyte. It was his testimony before a House committee in 1978 that I read as a Senate staffer that first introduced me to the idea of employee ownership. I was hooked from then on. Soon after, I journeyed to Cornell to meet Bill, not without some trepidation. He was, after all, one of the country's best-known scholars and the former president of the American Sociological Association. I needn't have worried. He was as gracious as he was insightful. His idea about "action research" in this subject was that it could, and should, be both academically rigorous and objective while at the same time moving the idea of employee ownership forward. It was that model that inspired the approach we have taken at the NCEO. Bill Whyte died some years ago, but I hope that some of his spirit still resides in me.

—*Corey Rosen*

As the person responsible for reporting and drafting much of this book, I am indebted to many people. My coauthors naturally shared their extraordinary expertise with me. Gina Malloy, Sam Case, and my longtime colleague Karen Carney helped me gather information about companies. Joseph Blasi helped me understand both the history of employee ownership and how to go about studying the subject. Several other experts in the field were kind enough to talk with me; the group includes Jeff Gates, J. Michael Keeling, Patricia Hetter Kelso, Norman Kurland, John Logue, Ron Ludwig, Chris Mackin, Alex Moss, Loren Rodgers, and Ryan Weeden. I am grateful to them all.

I am especially grateful to the many remarkable people in the employee-owned companies I visited who gave up part of their workday to answer my questions and share their experiences. I'll do my best to list them all here, and if I have inadvertently left anybody out, I am truly sorry.

CPES: Bob Bennetti, Cindy Gallon, Shannon Hartman, Steve Ross, Amy Rubinson, Tom Schramski, Greg Stewart. Gardener's Supply: Sherry Ceresa, Wyatt Christman, Jim Feinson, Todd Fisher, Dalton Flint, Tim Lewis, Will Raap, Cindy Turcot. W. L. Gore & Associates: Jim Buckley, Burt Chase, John Czerwinski, John Dennison, Robert McCracken, Ed Schneider, Holly Williams. Green Mountain Coffee Roasters: Kathy Brooks, Sherwood Brown, Robin Ferris, Roger Garufi, Randy Lewey, Sarah Patterson, Winston Rost. Jackson's Hardware: Karen Adolphson, Robert Akins, Carolyn Emge, Steve Graham,

Mark Helm, Steve Hossfeld, Bill Loskutoff, Matthew Olson, Suzy Tevini. King Arthur Flour: Cindy Fountain, Jeffrey Hamelman, Jane Korhonen, Cindy Johnson, Jay Rimmel, Frank Sands, Heidi Skilling, Steven Voigt. McKay Nursery Company: Tom Buechel, Guillermo Castillo, Jerry Draeger, Tim Jonas. Nypro: Al Cotton, Brian Jones, Rich Landry, Gordon Lankton, Karen Schomacker, Sue Sheridan. Phelps County Bank: Julie Bell, Peggy Laun, Bill Marshall, Wendy Young. SAIC: Emily Carbone, Karen Garsson, Steve Rockwood, Bill Scott, David Snyder, Joseph Walkush, John Warner. Scot Forge: Tom Allison, John Cain, Rick De Rosa, Jennifer Herman, Becky Iden, John Kasprzak, Mike Klingenberg, Leo Szlembarski, Paul Szymanski, John Wegener, Karen York. Stone Construction Equipment: Burt Farley, Bob Fien, Stanley Gerhart, Freddy Johnson, Dick Nisbet, Nancy Scharlock, Scott Woodruff, Lynne Woodworth. YSI: Rosalie Catalano, Cindy Ferguson, Lynn Livesay, Mark McCue, Susan Miller, Rick Omlor, Jill Riley, Deb Stottlemyer, Harriet Sweet, Diana Tillman.

Other people from employee-owned companies who provided information and insights for this book include Steve Ellinwood and Margie Karps, BMD (Building Materials Distributors); Bill Carris and Karin McGrath, Carris Companies; Keith Robertson and Dennis Zimmerman, ComSonics; Dan Bannister, formerly of DynCorp; Ed Zimmer, ECCO (Electronic Controls Company); David Knutson, Farmers National Company; Brenda Blair, Hypertherm; Jim Grenier, Intuit, Inc.; Michael Dougherty and Scott Kinsey, Kindermusik International; Kim Jordan, New Belgium Brewing Company; Will Kuchta and Laura Saxby Lynch, Paychex; Karen Aasen, Thoits Insurance Service; Sheryl Neuman, Toll Company; and John Mock, Travel and Transport. Many thanks to them all.

Actually producing a book, of course, requires collaboration of many sorts, and not just between the authors and the people they write about. I appreciate the efforts of Daniel Greenberg of Levine/Greenberg Literary Agency and Melinda Merino and her colleagues at Harvard Business School Press, all of whom helped get this book into print in the best possible shape. And I particularly appreciate the financial support provided by the National Center for Employee Ownership, by Ray Smilor and the Beyster Institute, and by the following individuals and organizations: Waite Dalrymple, Employee Ownership Foundation; Donald Israel, Benefit Concepts Systems, Inc.; David R. Johanson, Johanson Berenson LLP; Jared Kaplan, McDermott, Will & Emery LLP; Leslie Lauer, Alliance Holdings, Inc.; Dennis Long, Principal Financial Group; Bill Loskutoff, Jackson's Hardware; Tony Mathews, Principal Financial Group; John D. Menke, Menke & Associates, Inc.; Michael Quarrey, FilmX Technologies; Hugh Reynolds, Crowe Chizek and Company LLC; Sid

Scott, Woodward Communications, Inc.; Ken Serwinski, Prairie Capital Advisors, Inc.; Robert W. Smiley Jr., Benefit Capital Companies, Inc.; Robert Strickland, Lowe's Companies, Inc.; and Duane Tolander, Corporate Continuity Group, Ltd. Without their support, this book would have taken much, much longer to complete. Indeed, it might never have been written at all.

Finally, as always, special thanks to Quaker Case, who saw the book through from conception to delivery.

—*John Case*

My contribution to this book would not have been possible without the help and influence of many special people who have exposed me to new ideas, challenged old ones, and presented living examples of practice and action. They have enriched my thinking and understanding and in that capacity are co-contributors to this volume.

The fact that the contribution of my coauthors is obvious does not mean that it should go unmentioned. John Case, whom I have come to know over the time that we have collaborated on this book, has delighted me with the power of his keen intelligence and subtle insight; his kindness, decency, and good humor; and a gift of communication that humbles those of us who thought they knew how to express themselves with the written word. He has displaced all predecessors as the most gifted writer I have had the privilege to work with in my lifetime.

I have known Corey Rosen for twenty years, since joining the NCEO in 1984. He has been like a lighthouse before the harbor, marking the way with an unfailing beacon through stormy weather and calm. It would be hard to imagine anyone writing any publication on the subject of employee ownership who would not list Corey Rosen among the first few names on the acknowledgments page. To my mind, his enduring and selfless dedication to public education about employee ownership represents the greatest contribution to the concept since the passing of Louis Kelso.

Thanks and appreciation also go, gladly and deservedly, to my comrades in arms in the employee-ownership cause at the Beyster Institute: Dana Cordero, Alisa McMillan, Debra Sherman, Ray Smilor, Georgeanne Smith, Maia Tomich, Peggy Walkush, Anna Wood-Vasey, and especially Ron Bernstein and David Binns, who have been there shoulder to shoulder with me since my first day there; the visionary group of business founders and leaders, only some of whom are named in this book, who have had the insight and courage to transform their organizations into "equity" companies, showing those of us who simply report on it how it is actually done; Dave Johanson, a true employee-ownership attorney who taught me the legal process; Bob Beyster, founder of SAIC, and a Level V Leader if there ever was one; and my parents, George and Sarah Staubus of El Cerrito, who blessed me not only with a pretty decent set of genes, but with an intellectual interest in how the world works and a sense of responsibility to try to make it better.

—*Martin Staubus*

INDEX

ABOUT THE AUTHORS

Corey Rosen is cofounder and Executive Director of the National Center for Employee Ownership, a nonprofit membership organization in Oakland, California, dedicated to providing objective, reliable information about broad-based employee ownership. One of the nation's foremost experts on the subject, he is author or coauthor of several books and more than one hundred articles on employee ownership, and is regularly quoted in the media. Earlier, Corey taught political science at Ripon College and worked as a professional staff member in the U.S. Senate, where he helped draft legislation on employee ownership plans. He holds a PhD in political science from Cornell University. The NCEO's Web site is www.nceo.org.

John Case is an internationally known writer on entrepreneurship and management. Author of five books and collaborator on three others, he has also written for many periodicals, including *Inc.* magazine and *Harvard Business Review*. He coined the term *open-book management* more than a dozen years ago and has written widely on the subject since then. At present John is a contributing editor at *Inc.* and a consulting writer for a variety of clients, including Bain & Company, the Business Literacy Institute, the Initiative for a Competitive Inner City, and the Great Game of Business.

Martin Staubus is Director of Consulting for the Beyster Institute (University of California, San Diego), a nonprofit organization that promotes entrepreneurship and employee ownership to build stronger companies. He has spent the past twenty years in the field of employee ownership, variously working as practicing attorney, corporate executive, and management consultant. He has also served as a policy analyst for Robert Reich, secretary of labor; legal advisor to the California State Labor Relations Board; and Deputy Director of the

ESOP Association. Martin is currently a member of the board of directors of the National Center for Employee Ownership. He holds an MBA in organizational development from George Washington University, Washington, D.C., and a law degree from Golden Gate University in San Francisco. The Beyster Institute's Web site is www.beysterinstitute.org.